WIRKSWORTH

A HISTORY

WIRKSWORTH

A History

Anton Shone and Mary Wiltshire
in conjunction with
Wirksworth Civic Society

First published in Great Britain in 2016 by

Bannister Publications Ltd
118 Saltergate
Chesterfield
Derbyshire S40 1NG

Copyright © Anton Shone and Mary Wiltshire

ISBN 978-1-909813-23-6

Anton Shone and Mary Wiltshire assert the moral right to be identified
as the authors of this work

A catalogue record for this book is available from the British Library

This book is sold subject to the condition that it shall not, by way of trade or otherwise, be lent, re-sold, hired out or otherwise circulated without the copyright holder's prior consent in any form of binding or cover other than that in which it is published and without a similar condition including this condition being imposed on the subsequent purchase.

All rights reserved. No part of this book may be reproduced or transmitted in any form or by any means, electronic or mechanical including photocopying, recording or by any information storage and retrieval system, without permission from the copyright holder, in writing.

Typeset in Palatino Linotype by Escritor Design, Chesterfield, Derbyshire

Printed and bound in Great Britain by SRP Ltd, Exeter, Devon

Acknowledgements

The authors would like to thank Bill Bevan, John Foxon, Barry Joyce, Iain MacKay, Anne Parker, Phil Richards, Tony Short, Jane Smith, Sue Woore, Derbyshire VCH Wirksworth group, the staff of the Derby City Local Studies Library and the Derbyshire and Lichfield Record Offices for their help with this publication.

... about the authors:

Anton Shone is an archaeologist with a keen interest in the history and development of the Kingdom of Mercia and its province of the Peak District. He has supervised a number of digs in and around Wirksworth during the last 10 years and has sought to illuminate the history of the town and its role in Mercia through archaeological fieldwork and investigation.

Mary Wiltshire has lived in the Wirksworth area for fifty years and has always had a keen interest in the town and its history. For the last ten years she has researched the landscape history of Derbyshire, publishing with others *Duffield Frith* and *Medieval Parks of Derbyshire*.

The cover is taken from *'Green Hill'*, an original watercolour, courtesy of Iain Mackay.

Contents

Acknowledgements v
Foreword ix
Introduction xi
Chapter 1: Pre-history to 1066 1
   Pre-history and the Surroundings of Wirksworth
      The Origins of Wirksworth 3
      'Lost Lutudarum' – Romans and Lead 4
      The Dark Ages 6
      A provincial town of the Mercian Kingdom 11
      The Wirksworth charter of 835 12
      Place-names 14
      Roads and Tracks 16
      The Viking Age 18
      The End of Mercia and the Beginnings of England 19
Chapter 2: 1066-1700 21
   The Norman Conquest and Domesday Book
      The Manor 23
      The Medieval Church 26
      The Growth of the Town from the Medieval Period 28
      The Manor Courts 31
      The Market Place and its Surroundings 32
      Medieval Streets and Burgage Plots 34
      Mills 36
      Component Settlements 37
      Steeple Grange 37
      Wash Green 38
      Gorsey Bank 38
      The Dale and Greenhill and later encroachments on the 'wastes and commons'. 38
      Bole Hill 40
      Who Lived in Wirksworth? 40
      Anthony Gell Grammar School 42

    The Almshouses..42
    Stuart Expansion..43
    The Old Manor House and the demolished Wirksworth Hall.......................44
    Hopkinson's House, 1-3 Greenhill..45
    Babington House, Greenhill...46
Chapter 3: 1700 to the Present Day..51
    Georgian Prosperity
    Symond's House, 15 Market Place..52
    The Gate House, the Causeway...54
    Hope and Anchor Public House..54
    Red Lion Hotel..54
    Nineteenth Century Industry...55
    Limestone Quarrying..58
    Dale Quarry..58
    Baileycroft Quarry..58
    Middlepeak Quarry (Bowne and Shaws, and Hopton Wood Stone)............59
    Coal Hills Quarry (Hopton Wood Stone)...59
    Colehill Quarry (Alfred Shaw)...59
    The Governance of the Town...61
    The Barmote Court...62
    Religion, Health, Education, Social Life and Local Customs........................64
    Twentieth Century Wirksworth...65
Conclusion..69
Further Reading and Information..70
    Websites..70
    Books...70
    Articles..70
    Documents..71
List of Illustrations..72
    Illustrations and Maps within the Text..72

Foreword

This book is the work of dedicated local historians, Mary Wiltshire and Anton Shone. They have freely given their time, academic knowledge and inspiration so that Wirksworth's place in English history has at last been recorded. A wealth of domestic detail, landmarks and signs from the past will take the reader through the town in both time and space. From the grand Georgian lawyer's house in the market place to the higgledy-piggledy worker's cottages clinging bravely to each other, Wirksworth tells its story.

Whether you are a first-time visitor to Wirksworth or have lived here all your life, possibly descended from a long line of hill farmers, quarrymen, lead miners or cloth-makers, you will be sure to find something in this book to inform, surprise and delight.

Jill Tait
Chair, Wirksworth Civic Society, 2016

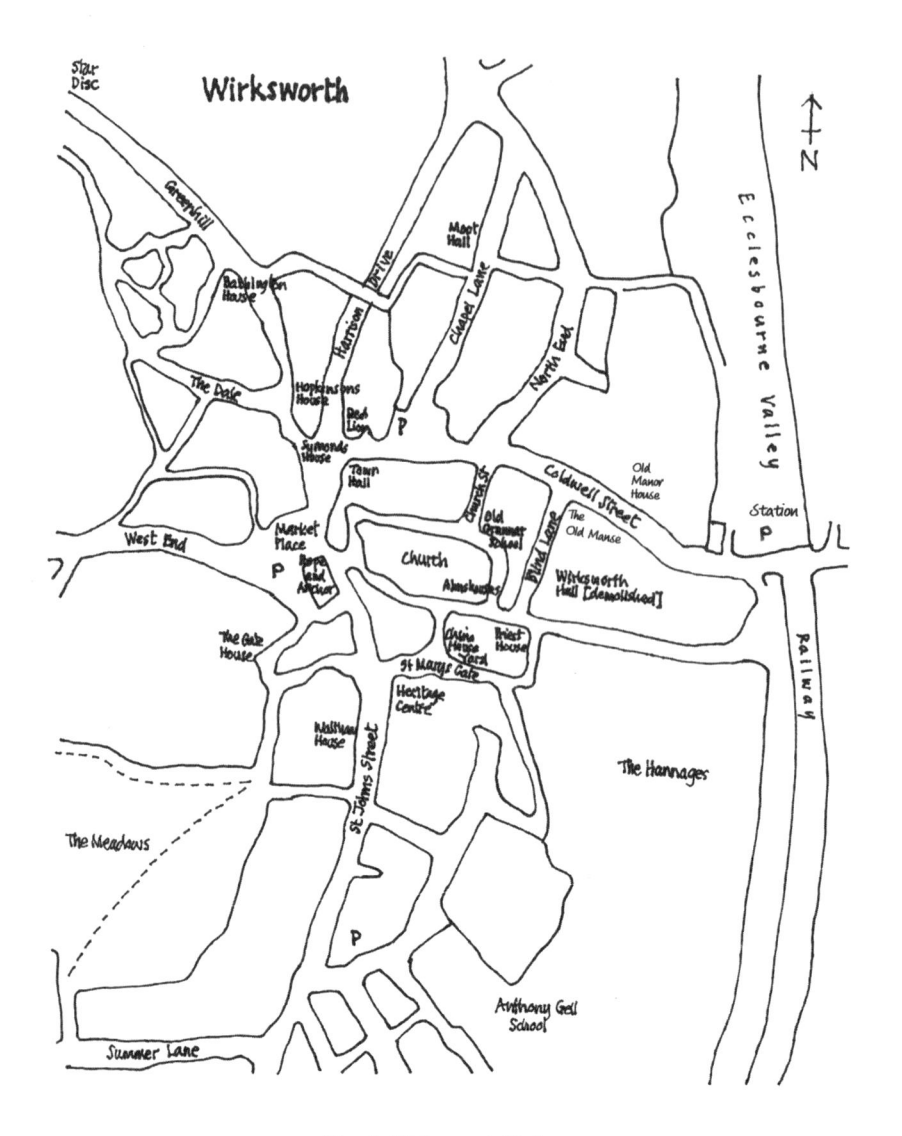

Map 1: Wirksworth Today

Introduction

"Wirksworth was a town when Canterbury was a village and Liverpool was a swamp" (Local saying)

THERE IS A measure of truth in this, for Wirksworth is the town in Derbyshire with the earliest surviving charter. Abbess Cynewaru, speaking twelve centuries ago in 835, calls us her *'villa'*, her town of Wirksworth. Being a town is in many ways an attitude of mind, that is to say the inhabitants of the settlement regard themselves as a town. This is certainly the case with Wirksworth, whose long-standing residents are firm in this belief: indeed many a newcomer has had their knuckles very severely rapped for using the word village when referring to Wirksworth.

This book is an attempt to unravel the history of this town. All such histories will please some people and annoy others. We have tried to include topics we felt would be of interest to most readers, both residents and visitors. It is clear however that much further research could be done to fill out some parts of the town's history and there is a wealth of information both archival and archaeological that still needs to be studied. New information will always come to light and Wirksworth's history will continue to evolve.

Chapter 1

Pre-history to 1066

Pre-history and the Surroundings of Wirksworth

THE WHITE PEAK, that is to say that part of the Peak District which is made up of the limestone plateau and on whose south eastern edge Wirksworth lies, is important in the development of the town because of the features which the geology and the topography contain. The centre of Wirksworth is built on the edge of the limestone plateau at the point at which the geology changes to gritstone and in the short boundary of the change between the limestone and the Ashover Grit, the town centre and Oat Hill also overlie shale bedrock covered in a layer of Clay Till. The Till is a heavy clay containing occasional pebbles. This influence of the limestone and gritstone can be also seen remarkably clearly when the local fields and their boundaries are studied. In Wirksworth itself and to the immediate north and west the field boundaries are made up of limestone dry stone walls. These are built of gathered stone from the fields themselves and most of these are a fairly recent result of land enclosures between 1600 and 1800. On the other hand, to the south and east of Wirksworth the gritstone landscape has its fields bounded by gritstone walls and many hedges, most obvious along the Ecclesbourne Valley which runs from Wirksworth south to Duffield.

Wirksworth stands at the centre of a landscape well-known for its ancient remains, although these remains are rather under-examined in archaeological and historical terms. In the countryside around Wirksworth there are many burial mounds or 'lows'. Some, mostly towards the north and west, have been examined and found to contain Bronze Age, Iron Age, Roman or early Saxon period burials. In the immediate area around the town are a number of these burial mounds, but none of them have been explored, examples are: Chewlow near Pitty Wood, Henlowe near Pratthall Lane, Crichlow at the north end of Chapel Lane, Pillow Butts on the west side of Derby Road at Oat Hill, Tatlow between Brassington Lane and Hopton Lane. More are suggested from old field names such as Highlow Furlong, Long Lowe, Beardingslowe, Brymmynglow and Ravenslowe near the town. Those burial mounds on the east and south sides of the town are the least recorded, they are often overlooked and rarely occur in assessments of the archaeological environment.

In those cases where this historic landscape has been carefully examined, the results have been both instructive and enlightening. Wigber Low, just such a burial mound, lies to the west of Wirksworth, a little south of Bradbourne. The low, on a summit of land overlooking the Havenhill Brook and the surrounding country, was first a settlement in the Neolithic period 5,000 years ago, from which pottery shards have been identified of that date. In those days Neolithic groups placed their dead on open platforms, to be carried away by birds and animals. The Neolithic funeral platform lies just below the low itself. The occupation continued into the Bronze Age and the low was built of a cairn of large limestone blocks in that Age, 3,500 years ago, with archaeologists finding jet beads and other Bronze Age materials in the low. The next archaeological evidence from the low comes in the form of Roman coins found at the low. These may not just be coin losses, but may perhaps represent small offerings. Finally, the low was re-used in a major way in the 600s, with a number of burials of an early Saxon kind inserted into the low with various grave goods. This kind of re-use of Bronze Age barrows in the Dark Ages is quite common in the Peak District. Much the same is probably true of the Tatlow barrows at Hopton Lane on the high ground to the west of Wirksworth, where there is also a megalith and where there were finds of burials and Bronze Age jet buttons by lead miners in 1828. It is not yet known whether there are any Roman or Dark Age associations at Tatlows, but the fields immediately to the east are curiously known as the Holy Lands.

Close to Wirksworth are a number of Roman farm and small settlement sites including at City Folds overlooking the Via Gellia, at Pearson's Farm north of Ryder Point and at a site near Great Mootlow, on the east side of the Chariot Way. These habitation sites must have had convenient access to a local market. The surroundings of Wirksworth have this unusual intensity of Roman finds and sites. To the west of Wirksworth at Shiningford Farm, now under Carsington Water, is a villa-farm site (a farmhouse), another with an aisled building at Roystone Grange by Ballidon and a possible settlement site may exist at Rainster Rocks by Brassington. A similar Roman villa-farm site was recently excavated overlooking the river Amber at Heage.

In terms of industry, at Kniveton, a little south of Wigber Low, are the remains of what is considered to be a Roman paint-making site. To the northwest near City Folds are the Roman marble quarries at Hopton Wood. This marble was used in the Roman baths at Godmanchester (*Durovigutum*) and is thought to have been transported there by water. If this were so it might imply that the Derwent was navigable in Roman times at least as far as Whatstandwell, where the road from Wirksworth on Longway Bank comes down the riverside. Certainly in later medieval times it is thought possible that the Derwent was navigable this far north. It was known, from the accounts of the Duchy of Lancaster Steward, William of Birchover, that lead was delivered by barge to Nottingham in 1322.

South and east of Wirksworth an intensity of Roman industrial sites are found. Quern making was carried out at Streets' Rough, Alderwasley and at Starbuck House at Blackbook, close to the possible Roman road from Wirksworth to Little Chester via Belper Lane End, Dalley Lane and North Lane and a crossing of the Derwent at Milford (Muleford in Domesday Book). On North Lane, near the former rifle range, a mid-second century Roman coin hoard was found in 1868, close to the Roman pottery kiln site at the Chevin Golf Course. Pottery making is found extensively between Wirksworth and Little Chester. There were further Roman kiln sites at Alport Height, in Shottle near the Hall and in Hazelwood, Farnah Green, Duffield and Holbrook. This is pottery making on an industrial scale and it has to be remembered that its success depends on the close proximity to its markets and the effectiveness of the road network to enable the finished pots to be transported to them.

The Origins of Wirksworth

The historic centre of Wirksworth lies on a rising tongue of land, bounded on the east side by the headwaters of the River Ecclesbourne and on the south side by the former course of the Warm Brook, at Water Lane. This probably resulted in a dry and defensible area for which water was readily available, both from these streams but also from a number of thermal springs. Nearby, then as now, the valley and its surroundings were wooded and this provided a convenient source of firewood. Once cleared of woodland there was space in which to farm. These are considerable advantages. The head of the valley in which Wirksworth rests also provides comparative shelter from the wind and weather of the limestone plateau and the surrounding hills.

The thermal springs in particular deserve attention as a possible reason for the origin of the settlement. It is necessary to look back into historic documents for evidence of this for these springs are now gone. The thermal issue is crucial for an effective settlement because it means that there is a reliable water supply in the winter. The hydrology of Wirksworth was drastically changed during the Jacobean and Georgian periods when many drainage soughs were built, destroying the thermal springs and the streams they fed. The first sough to be constructed was the Dovegang Sough, started in 1632, and the later Hannage Sough started in 1693. The Hannage Sough and its later branches did much of the damage. A good example of this loss is the Warm Brook, which ran along the south side of Water Dale, now called Water Lane, where its course is completely obliterated. Similarly springs which rose in the churchyard and in many places around the town were destroyed by the sough-making. Thomas Bagshaw, a local lawyer much involved in litigation about the soughs said, in 1702: 'the town of Wirksworth hath borne the losses of their water from the town to the impairing of their health, being utterly deprived by the sough of as fine springs in the town as the Kingdome had'.

However, at the time of the origins of the settlement, these springs and streams and the defensible, easy to work, sheltered tongue of land would have been important. The early development of Wirksworth is neither well researched nor yet well understood and it is not until the Roman period is reached that we begin to get hints of how Wirksworth may have developed more rapidly, not only because of the advantages of its position, but because of its proximity to the lead deposits which occurred in the Limestone plateau. It is possible then, but not yet evidenced, that an Iron Age settlement may have been present on the tongue of land here. This, as well as the presence of thermal springs and something to trade, would have been important to the Romans in looking for a settlement or fort site from which to develop the economy of the district. Recent evidence for late Iron Age – Roman trading in the district comes for the coin hoard found at Reynards Cave in Dovedale in 2014. This coin hoard included both Iron Age coinage and early Roman coinage.

'Lost Lutudarum' – Romans and Lead

Much is known of Roman activity in the Peak. This is bound up with the development of the lead industry and the 'lost' Roman settlement of Lutudarum.

The most famous locally related Roman epigraphic inscriptions are those found on lead ingots. Chief amongst these is that found at Cromford Nether Moor in 1777 which was inscribed "IMP CAES HADRIANI AUG MET LVT" (Property of the Emperor Hadrian Augustus from Lutudarum) so dating it from between AD 117 to AD 138. It is the earliest datable Roman item found nearby, although Roman pottery has been found in the town itself at St Mary's Gate, in the Great Hannage and at Pittywood Road. A copy of this lead ingot can be seen at the Wirksworth Heritage Centre.

A late second century Roman coin hoard was found in 1735, allegedly near the Blobber Mine on the west side of Swaines Meadow by Summer Lane, with 83 Roman silver denarii ranging from Emperors Augustus to Lucius Verus. A denarius would be the equivalent of a day's pay for a soldier or a skilled person, say about £80 now, so this hoard would amount to having about £6,600 in the bank. The range of coins in the hoard would reflect the type of coins in circulation at the time the hoard was hidden. The last coins of Lucius Verus give an approximate date for the deposition of the hoard of (at the earliest) 161 when Lucius became emperor and not much later than 169, as the hoard would have had to contain coins in circulation of Marcus Auralius or Commodus to be later. This coin hoard is often overlooked but is significant because of its value, that is to say it contained silver coinage. Many of the other better known, and sometimes larger coin hoards found locally, such as the Cromford coin hoard of about 1795, the Scarcliffe Hoard of 1876 or that found recently near Heage in 2012 are either of copper or brass coins or barbarous radiates ('emergency coinage') of low denominations. Perhaps the closest comparator to the Wirksworth Hoard is the Parwich Hill hoard of 1769 in which 79 denarii were found, and whose date of deposition is strikingly similar.

The presence of *Lutudarum* as a Roman lead mining centre, a provincial administrative capital and a market place in the Peak is well attested. The later record of Roman towns and fortresses across the empire, known as the Ravenna Cosmography, lists *Lutudarum* in the same geographical area with *Veratino* (Rocester) and *Derbentione* (Little Chester, Derby). Yet here lies a conundrum, for Lutudarum has long been thought lost and the antiquarians and historians of Derbyshire over the last 300 years could, for the most part, barely bring themselves to acknowledge that Wirksworth might be a candidate for that place. If indeed Wirksworth does prove to be lost *Lutudarum* it will be through the efforts of archaeologists and these efforts have only recently begun. The most recent developments in this field have been the understanding that the Roman road to Buxton, known as 'The Street', starts at Wirksworth and the Roman road to Brough on Noe, known as 'The Derbyshire Portway' also starts at Wirksworth and runs out of the town along West End and then in the course of Brassington Lane.

The Dark Ages

The Dark Ages present a conundrum; they are a turning point in history and one which is poorly understood. At the end of the Roman age the Roman army was withdrawn in 410 and Britain left to look after itself, but this was at the time thought to be temporary: the army would come back. It never did. What then happened was a long and relatively slow conquest of Roman Britain by the invading Saxons which was complicated by the presence of different groups in different parts of the country. Some of these groups e.g. the Saxons, were certainly intent on conquest, but some of them, such as the Mercians, appear originally to have been the allies of the Romano-British. The Mercians were settled around the valley of the River Trent at Repton and other nearby places and their role seems to have been to guard the Trent Valley and the Rossington Gap as federates (allies) of the Romano-British. 'Mercian' means 'Borderer'. For two hundred years peace prevailed as far as we can tell in the Peak, the former Roman province of the Lutudarenses. However in the early 600s another group started to make their mark: the Northumbrians. The Northumbrians defeated the Romano-British and their allies at the Battle of Chester in 616 and by this means the Northumbrians gained control of virtually everything north of the Trent including the Peak.

What happened then is very curious. The British with the Mercians waged a long war to recover the Peak District from the Northumbrians. There were many battles and Cadwallon of the British and the early kings of Mercia, Penda, Wulfhere and Ethelred made repeated and determined attempts to eject the Northumbrians from the Peak, which they eventually achieved at the Battle of the Trent in 679. This is the point at which the Mercian kingdom becomes important in the history of Wirksworth and when Wirksworth becomes part of Mercia. Often sources are in Welsh and many place-names subject of conjecture by historians lacking knowledge of the geography of the Mercian-Northumbrian war and of the Peak and its surroundings, making understanding difficult.

This brings up the question of what happened to the *Lutudarum* place-name and its unproven location despite all recent archaeological efforts. Lutudarum means

"Grey Oakwood". In the Ravenna Cosmography, *Lutudarum* is recorded as a significant place. In the Dark Ages there is a more Welsh version of the name: Caer Lwytgoed, sometimes written Lwytcoed or Lwytkoed. This means fortification *(caer)* of the grey *(lwyt)* wood *(goed)*. This name was recorded by Welsh sources and, in one of the battles in 636, Penda and others defeated the Northumbrians at Caer Lwytcoed, took a great deal of plunder from the place and killed a bishop during the attack. This battle is almost always reported to be at Lichfield, probably a nonsense given any modern understanding of the geography of the Mercian – Northumbrian war.

It is possible that the Northumbrians were using the place-name simply as Ludeu, a kind of spoken shortening of the Welsh name, and this occurs in some further sources, such as Nennius. To make understanding more difficult, the Venerable Bede, in his History of the English Church and People, (Historia Ecclesiastica Gentis Anglorum) effectively a Northumbrian source and in Latin, reports some of these battles. His references to the Mercian-Northumbrian war are quite confused, resulting in years of historians reading Bede and thinking the Mercians were somehow in Stirling in Scotland. This failure to get it right results in historical and antiquarian sources which say that one minute Penda is fighting a war in Lichfield and the next minute he's fighting a war in Stirling, when all the time he may well be struggling with his appointed task: to eject the Northumbrians from Wirksworth and the Peak District, a task which Wulfhere continued and which Ethelred succeeded in achieving in 679.

If Wirksworth proves to be this place then it is perhaps possible that the Wirksworth Stone commemorates the death of the bishop. Understanding Dark Age sources is not helped by different names being used for what may be the same place by the different groups involved. The Mercians called the place Wirksworth, but that doesn't mean *'fortification of the grey wood'*. What Wirksworth means is the subject of another discussion (see below). These things said, it is just possible that Lwytcoed or Ludeu are faintly remembered locally, for there was a Ludwell in old documents and there still is a field called Lydia Flatts overlooking the town from the west of the valley near Summer Lane.

Nevertheless it is one of those curiosities of history and archaeology that it is only when the so called 'Dark Ages' are reached after the end of Roman rule, it begins to be obvious the settlement of Wirksworth was important in a major way. To see this it is necessary to understand the beginnings of St Mary's church and its role as a minster church. Firstly it has to be remembered that the late Roman Empire was Christian and its provinces often corresponded with the dioceses of the church. Secondly that even where the civil government of a Roman province failed or was overwhelmed by invading Saxons, the governance of the church did not fail. This tells us about continuity.

Evidence, some circumstantial and some material, has pointed to the early establishment of a church here in Wirksworth. From the 7th century Christian Mercian kings spread Christianity and built minster churches on royal estates, Wirksworth being one such. If we take the view that the early Christian community established in this Romano-British lead mining area survived the social and economic disruption of the post-Roman era, then it is perhaps the only Derbyshire settlement site at which Christian worship has been maintained since Romano-British times without a break. Well-known ancient sculpture within the church and churchyard also attest to this early establishment, particularly the Wirksworth Stone, a Northumbrian sarcophagus lid. The ancient ecclesiastical parish included dependant chapelries at Bonsall, Carsington, Kirk Ireton and possibly Matlock at the outset, together with the area of Alderwasley, Ashleyhay, Ible, Middleton and Hopton.

Something to see at St Mary's Church:

The Wirksworth Stone

In 1820, during building work, a stone grave vault with an upside-down but close-fitting lid covering a large skeleton was found under the church floor in front of the altar. The location close to the altar suggests a person of very holy status. The Stone, still in the church, is an extremely rare and fine example of early religious funerary sculpture, it is Wirksworth's greatest treasure. The

Wirksworth Stone has been very extensively studied, but these studies have tended to concentrate on the iconography of the Stone, what its pictures mean, not on what it represents in historical terms.

What does this tell us about St Mary's Church? Most significantly it suggests that St Mary's was no ordinary church, it was sufficiently important for a burial of the very highest status, perhaps a venerated holy person. For the Stone is indeed wonderful, for its time it is a piece of the highest art achievable. For this church to be built at all and to be endowed with such glory it had to be in a place able to afford its building and maintenance and to serve a large area. The dating of the stone causes the most difficultly, for it is unique. It has been compared on the one hand with Northumbrian stone carving of the seventh century and on the other hand with the sarcophagus of the Twelve Apostles in the church at Classe in Ravenna, dating from the fifth century, with which it bears distant similarities in terms of the bas-reliefs of its figures.

St Mary's Church also contains many other examples of Mercian and later stone sculpture built into the church walls. A few pieces of these sculptures are from cross-shafts and although many of the sculptural fragments can be found inside the church, one of the important fragments is built into the exterior: high up on the north choir aisle wall is a piece of knot-work from a Mercian cross. It has considerable similarities to the cross at Leek and to the north face of the cross shaft at St Peters church in Hope.

These sculptural fragments, taken together with the Wirksworth Stone, may imply the presence of a monastery or abbey in Mercian times, whose foundation was very ancient. For it should be borne in mind that St Chad, Bishop of the Mercians until 672, was according to the Welsh Annals, the Bonedd y Saint, the son of Cadvan, and here again there may, perhaps, be another faint reverberation of the Lwytcoed name: 'Siatt o Redynvre ap Cadvan Lwytcoed' (Chad of Fern Hill, son of Cadvan Greywood). This might imply something of St Chad's origins and his suitability for the post of Bishop of the Mercians. He may have accommodated the interests of all the parties involved, even the Northumbrians, for he spent time in Northumbria and Ireland before returning to Mercia. St Chad had three brothers and all played important roles in the development of the church at that time and this may also throw a light on the Wirksworth Stone and its possible date.

For information about the church and opening times see:
www.wirksworthteamministry.co.uk

Many early churches like the church in Wirksworth are named for St Mary. She was a cult figure in late Roman and early Mercian times, as was St Helen. Indeed

St Helen's name also occurs in Wirksworth, being one of the chantries of the church (see below). St Helen, mother of Constantine the Great, was closely associated with water and wells and, according to recent academic work, with Royal Mercian sites. Above Wirksworth on the east side of the town at the top of Wash Green is St Helen's Lane. It runs next to the spring line whose waters supplied and still supply Wirksworth with fine, clear, soft water from the springs at Breamfield. This sunken Lane was the 'ancient way to Derby' in the days before the turnpike roads and leads up to Alport Height, past the Roman pottery kiln site there and so on to Duffield via Spout and Shottle.

A short distance from St Mary's church is Wirksworth Heritage Centre. For the person interested in history, family or local, it is an important stopping off point. It holds many local artefacts, one of the smallest is the Wirksworth Sceat, a tiny coin, a penny, from long ago

Something to see in the Wirksworth Heritage Centre:

The Wirksworth Sceat

The Wirksworth Sceat was found by metal detectorist Cath Housley, lying on the spoil heap of an archaeological dig in Church Street in 1986. These coins are very rare and were made in the Kingdom of Northumbria and date from about 750AD. The picture above shows both sides of the Wirksworth Sceat. On the one side is a running horse or stag and on the other is the name of the king of Northumbria from 737 to 758, King Eadberht.

The Sceat is about the size of a modern 5p piece, a tiny object, but hugely informative about Wirksworth. This is because coinage of the time is very rare and this particular type of coin is rarer still and tends to be found outside Northumbria, only in locations with major churches or abbeys. This tiny find therefore supports the view that Wirksworth was a major ecclesiastical centre in the age before the Vikings.

For information about the Heritage Centre see:
www.storyofwirksworth.co.uk

A provincial town of the Mercian Kingdom

It might be thought from these archaeological finds that Wirksworth was part of Northumbria, but except for a short period between 616 and 679 it was not part of that kingdom, but part of the Kingdom of Mercia, the largest of the Saxon kingdoms. Indeed, because of the presence of the Great Barmote Court in Wirksworth (now the court of lead mining), Wirksworth was possibly the capital of the Mercian province called the Pecsaete, that is now called the Peak District. In today's world many people wrongly believe that the historic Peak District means the Peak District National Park. The Peak, homeland of the *Pecsaeten* (the 'Peak People'), as a province of the Kingdom of Mercia covered the entirety of later Derbyshire, the western half of Nottinghamshire as far as the River Idle, the north eastern part of

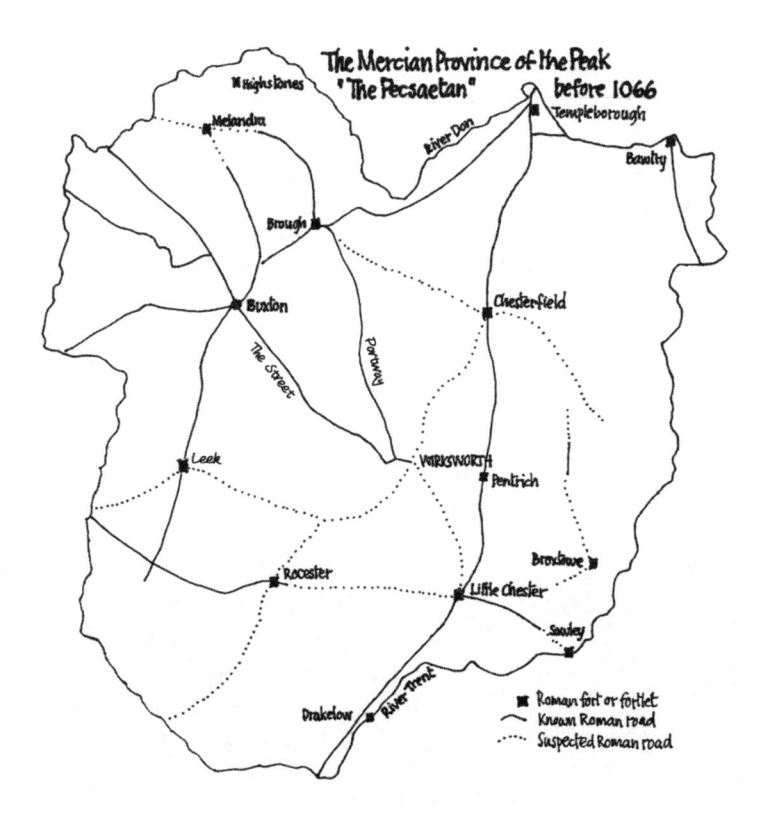

Map 2: The Mercian Province of the Peak

Staffordshire and the south eastern part of Cheshire, a huge area. It was administered by a governor, an Ealdorman, in the same way as the other ten principal provinces of Mercia.

The role of the Great Barmote Court of the Soke and Wapentake of Wirksworth, a rather cumbersome title, is to deal with matters of lead mining justice and this has been the case since the first known enquiry into its role in 1288, when it was described as being of 'great antiquity'. It would appear that the provincial capitals of the Mercian kingdom all had these courts. The modern Barmote Court now sits in a small courthouse, the Moothall, on Chapel Lane and is the oldest surviving court of its kind in Britain.

During the Mercian age a better picture of Wirksworth emerges and, for the first time, the name of someone directly associated with the town, the Abbess Cyneuuaru. She appears in the oldest written charter recording any town in the Peak, for in 835 she was compelled to give up some of her lands around 'her township of Wirksworth' to Duke Humbert of Tamworth. She does not appear to do so gladly, for the charter damns the Duke to become a friend of the Devil if he did not make an annual lead payment to Canterbury Cathedral.

The Wirksworth charter of 835

"In the year of the Incarnation 835, I Cyneuuara, Abbess, grant to Humbto, Duke, jurisdiction of land in my possession at Wirksworth, on condition that he shall give an annual render of lead to the value of 300 shillings to Ceolnoth, Archbishop and his successors [at Christ Church, Canterbury]. The above-named church should have this gift of mine from my aforesaid township every year. But if anyone should take away this my gift from Christ Church, Canterbury, may he be smitten with perpetual anathema, and may the devil possess him as one of his own."

The Wirksworth charter of 835

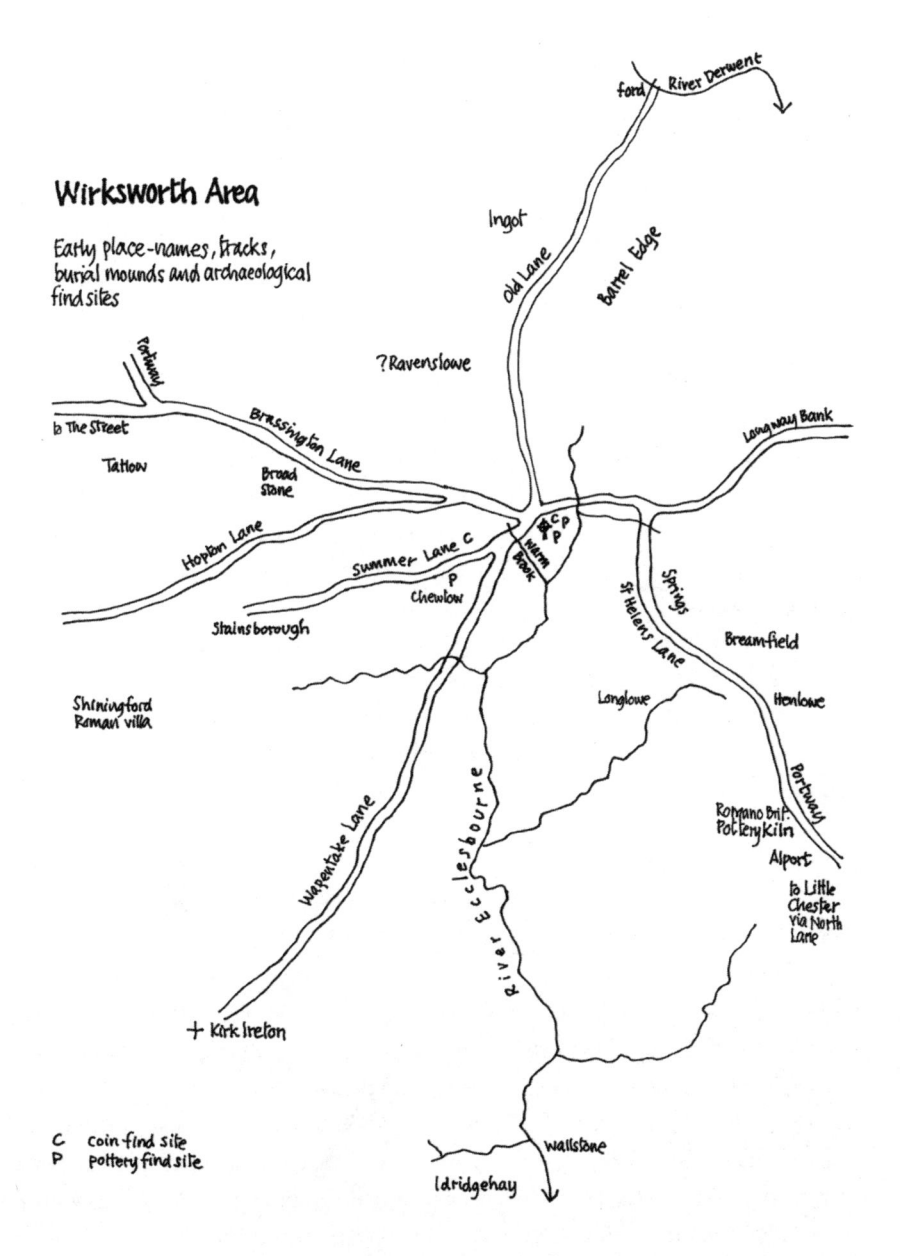

Map 3: Wirksworth Area, showing early place names, tracks, burial mounds and archaeological find sites

Place-names

The survival of place-names and their original meanings is often a cause of considerable interest to many people, indeed Wirksworth and its surroundings are said to boast more Celtic or British place-name survivals than some whole counties in the south of England. For example, overlooking Wirksworth is Barrel Edge, which is a compound of the Celtic *barr*, meaning hilltop, and the English *hill*: Barrhill> Barrel>Barrel Edge. However, the most important of these relates to the small river which meanders down the valley south of the town, the Ecclesbourne. *Eccles* is the Roman and Celtic word for church and *bourne* the word for stream or small river. This river has Wirksworth church at its head and Duffield church close to where it flows into the Derwent. The antiquity of this river name again alerts us again to the likely presence of St Mary's church in very ancient times.

Place-names are not always what they seem however. An example is Summer Lane, a small lane which runs into Wirksworth from Stainsborough. In old lead mining maps it is shown as a 'Roman old road'; it appears to be anything but this, and perhaps in this case the Roman appendage originates in the Roman coin hoard found in 1735. Summer Lane might be considered to be a lane usable only in summer, but the lane appears equally usable in winter. An alternative explanation of the place name is that Summer Lane might be a corruption of Sumpter Lane. A sumpter is the driver of a packhorse, originating in the Latin *saumatiarius*. Given the nature of Summer Lane this would make more sense, as Summer Lane effectively acts as a bypass from west to east around the edge of the town: taking pack animals through the town itself would raise a toll and using Summer Lane and its continuation Water Lane would avoid paying this.

Returning to the Ecclesbourne Valley there are many examples of what might be regarded as the integration of the Romano-British people with the incoming Saxons. Overlooking Wirksworth on the east side is Breamfield, a corruption of the place-name Brefield, meaning the 'fields of the British'. A similar place-name near Idridgehay, Wallstone Farm, has nothing to do with walls or stones, but means 'farm of the Welsh', again the Romano-British in fact. Idridgehay itself is very interesting, meaning the Hay or small enclosure belonging to Eadric, a man with a Saxon name, Eadric's Hay. There is an interesting walk through the village of Idridgehay around the Hay, whose earthworks can still in part be seen.

The Portways include the element *port*, and this place name relates to roads and trackways, in effect meaning 'main road' (road to a market town). It occurs in old documents and charters and in local place names where the word Portway appears or where the word *port* is part of something similar, such as the field name Portcliff in a rental document of 1415. Alport Height, for example, to the south east of Wirksworth, has fine views over many counties but its place-name suggests there was a Portway nearby. This might either be the road leading to North Lane mentioned earlier, which passed Alport Height on its eastern side, or it might refer to the road from Wirksworth to Shottle and Duffield via Spout, a reliable water source, which passes over Alport Height on its western flank.

Wirksworth: The Place-name

The charter from 835 quoted earlier is the first written reference to Wirksworth that has been found. Important consideration must be given to the meaning of the Wirksworth place-name and here the inadequacy of the knowledge about the origins of the town is evident. In Professor Kenneth Cameron's three volumes on 'The Place-names of Derbyshire' he identifies two elements in the name, *weorc* (a personal name, the first element) and *worth*, (meaning an estate or enclosure, the second element). To explain this first element he quotes previous 1940s work suggesting there was a Saxon person named Weorc. However, a great deal of research has been done on Saxon names in the 75 years since then. There is now a large database of Saxon names created by the University of Cambridge from surviving Saxon charters and old documents. The university found 112 references to the name *Eadric*, as in Idridgehay, but none whatsoever for anyone called *Weorc*. This lack of a proven personal name for the first element of 'Wirksworth' is important when interpreting the meaning of the place-name. Modern academics regard the assumption of personal names as being unlikely for those place-names originating before 900 and regard place-names prior to 900 as tending to be the result of references to geographical or physical features. It is therefore necessary to note that the name Wirksworth was in use by 835 as shown by the charter quoted above.

The alternative is that the *weorc* in Wirksworth meant 'fortification', literally a work or building, a meaning Cameron suggests but dismisses. This interpretation is the only one given for *weorc* when found in place names by A. H. Smith in his 1956 'Place Name Elements' published for the English Place Name Society. If this is the case Wirksworth may have meant 'fortified estate/enclosure'. The present state of archaeology in Wirksworth can throw no light on this, all that can be said is that this is work in progress. To muddy the waters further *weorcs* may be the plural of *weorc*, fortification, that is to say there was more than one fortification.

It is still undecided what the Wirksworth place name really means, but at the time of writing, it is looking less likely that Wirksworth means the estate of a person called Weorc and more likely that it perhaps means 'fortified estate or enclosure'.

Roads and Tracks

Lead remained important from the Roman period right through the Dark Ages to the Mercian age and almost to the modern day due to its many uses: lead pipes, coffins, baptismal water tanks and lead sheeting. Transport was needed to get lead from the mines and the smelters around Wirksworth to its markets. When looking at the road and trackway network around Wirksworth it becomes obvious that the town lies at the centre of a large network of Portways. Many of these Portways were based on the Roman road network, for Wirksworth can boast connections to Buxton and to Brough on Noe and probably to Little Chester near Derby by Roman roads. However, Roman roads in the Peak are not straight as they are in the lowlands of England, they twist and turn to accommodate high hills and steep gradients. Most lead was transported on the backs of pack horses and this was the case from the Roman period right through almost to the end of the lead industry in the Victorian age. The use of packhorses might have been one stage in a longer journey also involving transport by water, which was often easier in past times.

Some of these roads and trackways still survive in their almost original condition, from the days before roads were covered in tarmac. Two of the most interesting are the Chariot Way and North Lane. The Chariot Way was part of the Portway, the Roman road from Wirksworth to Brough on Noe, and only a short section of it now remains between the quarries at Bonemill at Ryder Point on Brassington Lane and Grangemill Quarry at Grangemill. It is difficult to reach except by footpaths, but is nevertheless popular with walkers. North Lane, west of Belper, is part of a packhorse

Brassington Lane, part of the Roman road from Wirksworth to Buxton and Brough, looking west

route connecting Wirksworth with Little Chester via a crossing of the River Derwent at Milford, once known as Muleford. North Lane can be walked from Farnah Green to Milford and has delightful views eastwards over the Derwent Valley. It is not known whether North Lane was Roman, for recent archaeological examination of it could find no evidence to date it. It does have a turf built edge unusual for a medieval road, turf revetment being a method used by Roman military engineers, and the lane has a Roman coin hoard associated with it mentioned earlier.

Roads or tracks came into Wirksworth from all directions but along the ridges not in the valley bottom. The ridge route to the south and east led from Wash Green up to Alport and by the 17th century, and probably earlier, was known as 'the way to Derby'. The bridge at the end of Coldwell Street was New Bridge in 1649 and from Anthony Gell's will, signed in 1579, we know it had been there some years earlier. A *Bridge Close* is noted on the later Tithe map 500 metres further south on the Ecclesbourne, close to where a path crosses the railway track, suggesting an earlier bridge was sited here. A 19th century newspaper article refers to 'a very old pack saddle bridge' being found at Wash Green, when the railway was built, and those having seen it having been strangely impressed by the quality of its construction.

Another route led south through Millers Green and up Wapentake Lane to Kirk Ireton. Old Lane led out of town northwards to Middleton and Cromford. West End led out of the town via Brassington Lane (known as High Street in 1613) north to Buxton, west to Brassington and north-west to Brough on Noe.

Within the town the historic street plan is still clearly visible today, the only disruption being the insertion of Harrison Drive in the late 1930s. Some names have changed, St. John's Street was for a time Nether Street and North End was North Town End. Coldwell Street and Warmbrook reflect two water sources in the town and The Causeway perhaps led over some boggy ground to Yokecliff but was known earlier as Gatehouse Street. Yokecliff Lane was formerly known as Wooley Lane, Wooley Green House was nearby (now called Buena Vista), possibly leading to 'wolf's clearing', or 'well clearing'.

The Viking Age

It is clear from the charter evidence and from the sculptural treasures in St Mary's church that Wirksworth was an important place before the coming of the Vikings. It is unlikely that such a place would be undefended and therefore another reason for archaeologists to redouble their efforts to find the remains of such fortifications, however fleeting. The main thrust of Viking attacks in the Peak District province of the Mercian kingdom came with the overwintering of the Viking great army at or near Repton in 873 in which they overcame King Burgred. The effect of this was the start of the settlement of many parts of north and eastern Mercia by the Vikings and the founding of Derby where a large detachment of the great army took root.

It is perhaps significant that they did not appear to settle in Wirksworth. Indeed Wirksworth may have long resisted them, in the same way that Leicester resisted them, for 17 years it is said. Eventually the Vikings of Derby and of several other towns were subdued by the combined forces of Mercia and Wessex. Derby surrendered to Aethelflaed, Lady of the Mercians in 917 and Edward of Wessex took Nottingham a year later. In 920 Edward, known as the Elder, took his army to Bakewell and built a fort nearby, a 'burg'. These efforts give every impression of a strategy not only to subdue the Vikings but also to secure Wirksworth and the valuable Peak District lead field from them. The success of this strategy shows in later place names, for those places with Viking or Danish associations often end in '*by*', hence Derby, Denby, Skegby etc. These are most common east of the Derwent but west of Wirksworth Danish place names are rare. The earlier Celtic and later

Anglo-Saxon place names survive, the latter often end in '*tun*', hence Carsington, Hopton, Kniveton etc. In addition to the military strategy to subdue the Vikings there was a strategy of recovering lands and estates from them by purchase in the Peak and other parts of Mercia. This is shown in a charter where land at Hope and Ashford was recovered by this means in 926.

Although Viking efforts to control much of England continued on and off right up until the Norman Conquest it is clear that Mercia and Wessex had prevailed. In Wirksworth, Viking influence appears to have been short-lived. There are a few indicators of life under the Danelaw: the appearance of the word 'Wapentake' instead of 'Hundred' for the administrative district and an occasional Danish place-name, unlike very many in the north-eastern parts of Derbyshire. The Viking legacy is more obvious by its absence than its presence around Wirksworth. The Peak continued as a province of Mercia until the end of that kingdom, although by now the emergence of shire counties begins to be seen as a means of gathering tax and manpower to support the *burgs* and keep the Vikings in check, and as a means of replacing the Mercian provincial administration.

The earlier name of Hamenstan Hundred, used in the Domesday Book for the Wirksworth Wapentake, harks back to the names of the English hundred meeting places. It relates to the organisation of law, order and taxation, hence Hamston, the old name for a gathering, as at Hamston Hill near Thorpe and the road leading there, Hammenstan Way at Carsington. The area of jurisdiction of the Wapentakes changed over time. Generally the words Wapentake and Hundred had fused together by the 10th century, but the continued use of both terms persisted until about 1800 in Wirksworth. The name Wapentake is still used locally for Wapentake Lane, or even 'The Wap', leading from Millers Green to Kirk Ireton. In 1415 John Helot is recorded as renting a 'messuage' (a house and associated buildings) and land in Wapentakfeld.

The End of Mercia and the Beginnings of England

One of the effects of the Viking wars was the emergence of England as a kingdom, and although there are many other reasons for this, the destruction wrought by the Vikings on the three constituent parts of England, the kingdoms of Northumbria, Mercia and Wessex, resulted in a period of change. The three former kingdoms flickered on and off for a while and then gradually became earldoms of the kingdom of England.

Mercia followed this pattern. After Aethelflaed, Lady of the Mercians, there were a number of Lords or Earls of Mercia and occasional rulers until finally in 959 the last King of Mercia, Edgar, became King of All England following the death of his brother King Edwig of Wessex. Edgar, known as 'the peaceful' was eventually crowned at Bath in 973: the coronation in those days was the culmination of a reign, not the start of one. It is in these later years that change is seen in the status of the Peak from a Mercian province to that of the shire counties. A charter issued late in this period for a land grant at Ballidon, a small village west of Wirksworth, mentions the Peak and dates from 963. It still retained the style and customs of the Mercian province.

This was the beginning of the creation of shire counties. It indicates the gradual dismemberment of the Peak Province into four parts, the central part into Derbyshire, the eastern part into some of Nottinghamshire, the south-western part into some of Staffordshire and the north-western part into some of Cheshire. Derbyshire is first mentioned in 1048 in the Anglo-Saxon Chronicle in relation to an *'earthquake in Derby-shire'*.

This dismemberment can still be found as an echo in the structure of Domesday Book almost 40 years later, after the Norman Conquest. The two shire counties of Derbyshire and Nottinghamshire are strangely lumped together and many historians, not understanding the history of the Peak, have found this inexplicable.

Above: Wirksworth at the head of the Ecclesbourne Valley.
Below: Wirksworth Church.

Above: Cottages on St.Johns Street, on possible medieval burgage plots.
Below: There has been a market in Wirksworth since the 13th century.

Above: Cruck frame of an earlier cottage hidden in later houses.

Below: Chemist's shop backing onto the churchyard.

Left:

Hopkinson's House,
1-3 Greenhill

Right:

The Dale

Right:
Cottages at Wash Green

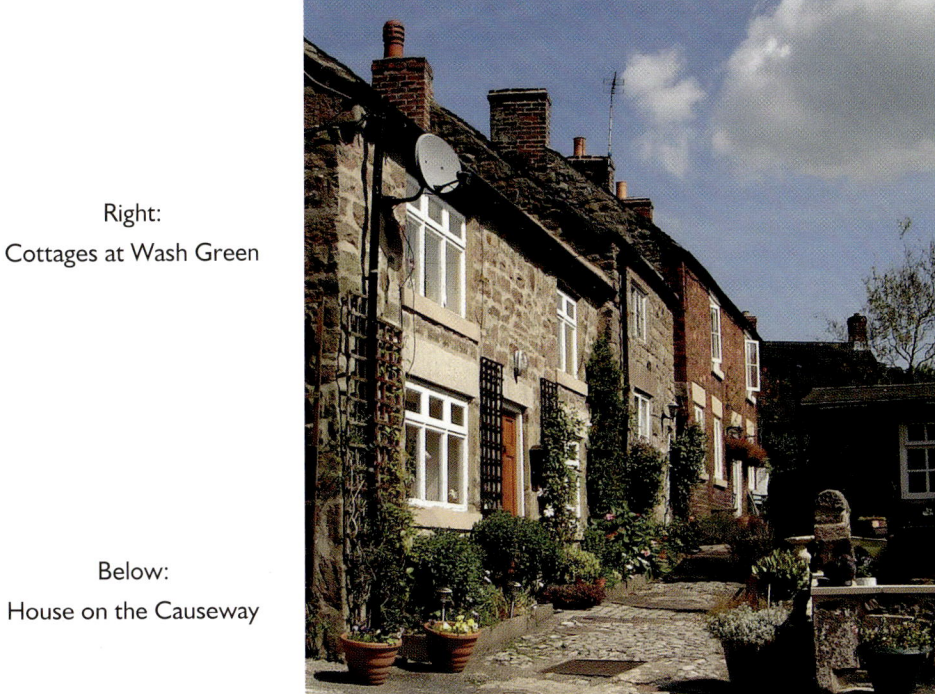

Below:
House on the Causeway

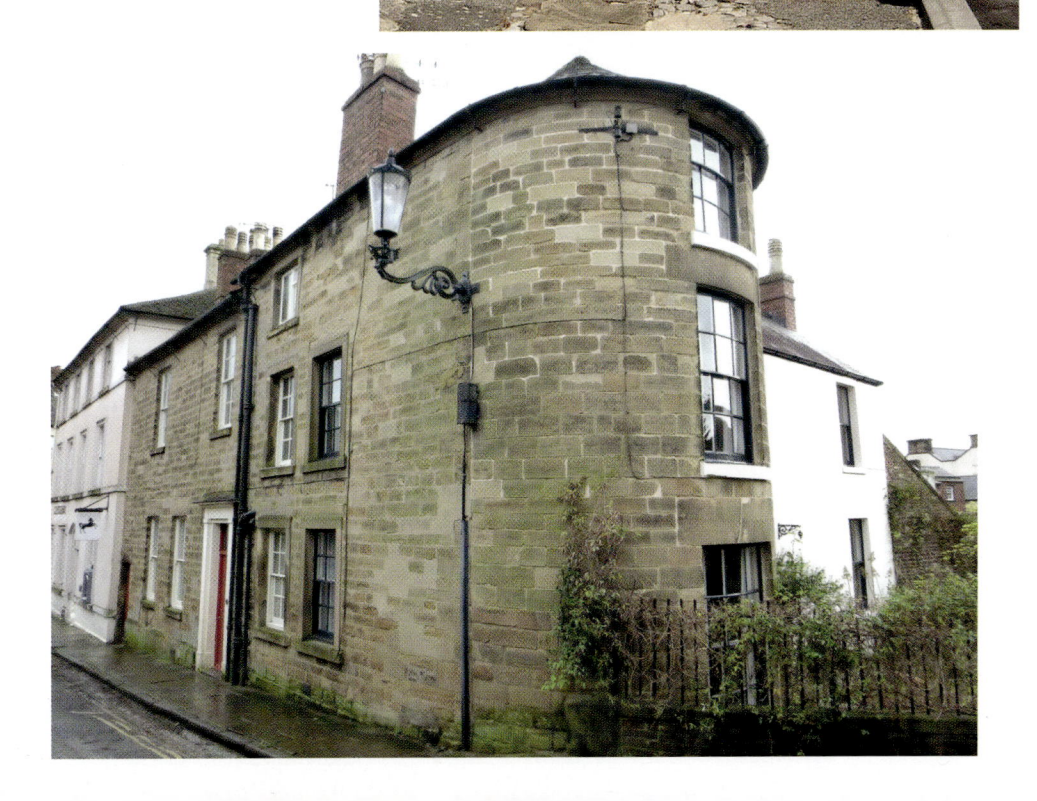

Left:
Old Grammar School

Below:
Looking up West End

Right:
Haarlem Mill

Below:
Middle Peak Quarry

Above: Entrance to Stoney Wood and Star Disc.
Below: Wirksworth Festival community music event.

Chapter 2

1066 - 1700

The Norman Conquest and Domesday Book

BEFORE THE NORMAN Conquest Edward the Confessor had held Wirksworth as one of several important groups of manors within the county. As with all such manors Wirksworth was a multiple estate with a central manor, a number of outlying hamlets serving the manor, a minster church and a land unit of great antiquity. This was the most archaic type of agricultural estate at the time and is often seen to have coincided with minster churches, as here.

King William succeeded Edward and personally held on to these wealthy manors in strategic positions within the county. The Wirksworth area of royal manors formed a buffer zone between the Derbyshire land of the Norman lords de Ferrers to the south and those of William Peveril to the north.

The Domesday Book is the most valuable record of life post conquest, seeking to establish the taxable value of the land and possessions. A basic structure of accounting and recording had already been in place in Anglo-Saxon times. By the 10th century the hierarchy in Derbyshire and Nottingham, run as a single shire, was that of a shire divided into wapentakes or hundreds, making the work of the Domesday scribes fairly easy; the whole took only two years to collect and collate all the material. Written in a shortened form of Latin it concisely gives a snapshot of life in England. It describes the manor of Wirksworth which at that time belonged to the King and had previously been held by King Edward.

Wirksworth in Domesday Book 1086

The King's land:
In Wirksworth there are 3 carucates of land. Land for 4 ploughs.
A priest and a church there, and 16 villagers and 9 small holders having 4 ploughs.
There are 3 lead works and 26 acres of meadow.
Wood, pasturable, 2 leagues in length and 2 leagues in breadth.

> Berewicks of this Manor.
> In Cromford 2 carucates, Middleton by Wirksworth 2 carucates, Hopton 4 carucates, Welledene* 2 carucates, Carsington 2 carucates, Callow 2 carucates, Ireton 4 carucates;
> 18 taxable carucates of land. Land for as many ploughs.
> In these there are 36 villagers and 13 smallholders, having 14 ploughs and a half.
> Meadow 14 acres
> Wood, pasturable, and underwood, 3 leagues in length and 2 in breadth.
> With Darley, Matlock, Ashbourne and Parwich, with their outliers, it paid £32 and 6½ sesters of honey before 1066; now £40 of pure silver.

A Carucate comes from 'carrucata' meaning a plough and was the area of land a team of 8 oxen could plough in a single season.
A League was about 3 miles or the distance a person could walk in an hour.
A Berewick was an outlying hamlet or village servicing the manor.
* Perhaps Dene Hollow between Carsington and Hopton or Willow Dean between Middleton and Cromford.

This gives a picture of a significant manor with seven outlying villages owing allegiance to it together with plenty of arable land, wood for pasturing stock and a small meadow. The importance of the church and the lead works has already been discussed. A priest's house stood, until the beginning of the twentieth century, at the corner of the churchyard and Blind Lane. Whether a medieval one stood on this spot is open to conjecture.

It is generally agreed that it is difficult to make an accurate population estimate from the Domesday Book. It was not a population survey but a tax and ownership document. The best that can be done is to make an estimate for the number of people by using a multiplier, usually six, the six being the villager or smallholder, his wife, say three offspring and one elderly parent and then adding 5% for slaves. This would give Wirksworth a population of 536. Using this multiplier other Derbyshire manors, later borough towns, would have had these populations in 1086: Ashbourne 208, Bakewell 340, Newbold with Chesterfield (one of its berewicks) 258, and Derby 1,027. These populations may seem low. Recent researchers have taken the view that the population multipliers typically used in the past for Domesday might be serious underestimates, a multiplier nearer 15 might be used. This would give the taxable population of Wirksworth in 1086 as perhaps 1,270.

The Manor

The settlement at Wirksworth would have been there to service this important royal manor with its 3 lead works. The land was divided into plough land, meadow for haymaking and pasture for grazing. The arable fields were divided into strips and villagers worked land spread throughout the town's fields usually in acre or ½ acre strips. These 'open' fields lay around the town and from later documents we know they were called North Field, between Wash Green and Bolehill, Dale Field, now mostly quarried away, and Bradstone Field between Brassington Lane and Hopton Lane. Oathill, Ryefield, Wheatcrofts and Barley Flats survive in field names and suggest a variety of crops being grown. Inhabitants would have been primarily engaged in agriculture with mining and quarrying of importance too. These inhabitants would have lived in small houses clustered around the church and market place.

The 14 acres of meadow listed in the Domesday Book could have been The Hannages. This is the area of land between Water Lane and north end of the Anthony Gell School playing field. The word comes from the old norse *'hegning'* and means 'enclosed land', that is the land that cattle were excluded from, possibly an ancient hay meadow. The name has been preserved in recent years by the naming of Hannage Way leading from Water Lane to the school playing field.

The woodland pasture and underwood would have been scattered throughout the area with parcels on the Gilkin, at Gorsey Bank and anywhere else where the topography made ploughing difficult. These places later became known as the 'wastes and commons' of the manor and were used by all tenants for the grazing of cattle, sheep and pigs.

In the 12th century the Stewards of the Manor were the de Ferrers family. Henry de Ferrers came over from Normandy at or soon after the Conquest and was rewarded for his loyalty with gifts of manors in fourteen English shires. In Derbyshire he had 101 manors, mostly grouped in the area south of Wirksworth. By some means the de Ferrers family became established as lords of the manor and the wapentake of Wirksworth, but, in a period of considerable unrest and political intrigue, the family enjoyed mixed fortunes. Over the next one hundred and fifty years the lordship of Wirksworth changed hands frequently between the de Ferrers and the Crown, as feudal loyalty faltered and at times erupted into open rebellion. A dramatic change occurred in 1269 when the rebellious Robert de Ferrers was disinherited of all his lands and properties. These then came into the hands of Edward, the elder son of King Henry III who became King Edward I, and later passed to his younger brother Edmund, the Earl of Lancaster. This may be a reason for the transfer of the church to the Dean of Lincoln in 1272 and the appointment of a new vicar. Edmund's lordship of these lands was established by decree in 1279 when there was a royal exchange of his counties and castles of Cardigan and Carmarthen for the king's manors of Wirksworth and Ashbourne, amongst other lands.

After the death of Edmund, Earl of Lancaster, in 1296-7 a brief snapshot of Wirksworth is given in his Inquisition Post Mortem. This was an inquiry into the lands held by deceased people of some status. The records survive in the National Archives at Kew. Among Edmund's lands Wirksworth was listed as having a capital messuage (main house), 100 acres of arable land, 23 acres of meadow, 24 shillings rent of free tenants by charter, 18s 3½ d rent of tenants without charter, 24 shillings from tenants of assarts (newly cleared areas), a fulling mill (for cleaning woollen cloth), a water mill, a market, a several pasture (a separately enclosed pasture), 13s 9d tallage (land tax) of tenants and 3 shillings for beaupleader (a court fine).

The 'capital messuage' or manor house for this manor was possibly on Coldwell Street either on the site of the Old Manor House or the site of the now demolished Wirksworth Hall. The fulling mill and water mill for corn grinding must have been on the Ecclesbourne River. It is possible the 'several pasture' listed here could have been a hunting park similar to the ones Edmund held in neighbouring Duffield Frith. An entry in court proceedings in 1281 clearly states that one was in existence: *'two unknown men were found killed in Lord Edmund's sheepfold in Wirkesworth Parke'*. Two fields bear the name Park on the Tithe Map of 1845, one near Hardhurst and the other near Breck Farm on Brassington Lane.

The manor continued to be held by the Lancasters, however upheaval still prevailed. After the execution of Thomas of Lancaster, Edmund's heir, Wirksworth was again briefly in royal hands. The Lancastrian estates then passed through marriage to John of Gaunt, who became Duke of Lancaster. During this time there was local unrest and disruption, with rebel attacks on the town and disruption to the market. John of Gaunt's son Henry Bolinbroke was crowned Henry IV in 1399. Thereafter the Duchy of Lancaster estates were vested in the crown and have been ever since.

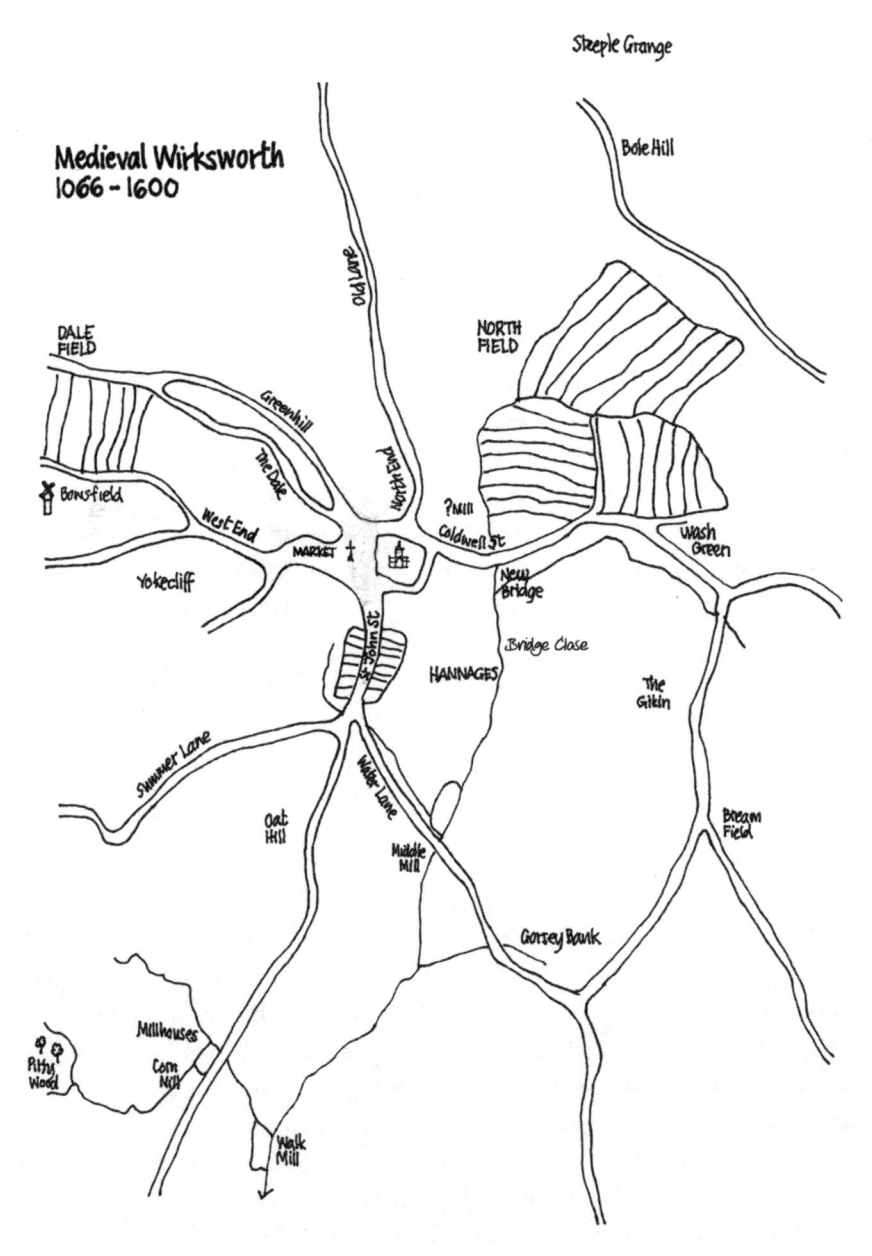

Map 4: Medieval Wirksworth

25

The Medieval Church

The early establishment of the church in Wirksworth has been discussed previously. By the high medieval period this minster church had dependent chapelries at Bonsall, Carsington, Kirk Ireton and possibly Matlock. All of these had become distinct parishes with their own rectories by 1291. Further chapelries were established within this large ecclesiastical parish, at Alderwasley by 1281 and Cromford by the early 16th century.

The church is of cruciform shape with a tower at the crossing. It is the widest church in Derbyshire and the third longest. Some of the lower fabric dates from 1272 when it is thought a major rebuilding took place in the Early English style. This is best seen in the lancet windows of the chancel and in the bases of the clustered piers of the central tower. A later development took place in the Decorated style, perhaps after 1300, when the tower was raised to its current height. The pointed two light window of the west end of the south aisle survives from this work, but without its original medieval stained glass. Work in the Perpendicular style took place about 1500 and this resulted in the battlemented parapets and crocketed pinnacles which adorn the exterior of the church.

In the late medieval period gifts to the church led to the establishment of a number of chantries, gifts to the church to ensure prayers were said for the soul after death. Chantries were abolished by Henry VIII following two acts of Parliament in 1545 and 1547. The records of these chantries in Wirksworth appear in various documents and old books. Some of them had small side chapels dedicated to different saints:

St Edmund's or the Blackwell Chantry was in the north transept. Richard Blackwell's will of 1505 stated that he wished to be buried before 'St Edmunds altar'. The 1524 will of Thomas Blackwell left money for masses to be said on alternate weeks, at St Edmund's altar and at St Mary's altar, as well as money for building (or perhaps rebuilding) of the north transept. The Blackwell brass, originally two memorials, survives on the wall of the north choir aisle and dates from 1525 and the Blackwell arms can be seen in the west window of the transept.

The Chantry of the Holy Rood or Chapel of the Holy Cross is in the south choir aisle. Originally the Chantry of the Vernons, it is mentioned in 1515 and was founded by Sir Henry Vernon and contained the raised tomb of Roger Vernon. This is recorded as having been 'lately removed' in 1710 to make space for some more

The churchyard in the 1950s

seats. It now contains the memorials of the Hurts of Alderwasley, of which the oldest dates from 1782.

St Catherine's Chantry in the south nave aisle on the west side of the tower was founded by the Wigleys of the Gate House. In 1540 Richard Wigley died and left instructions to be buried 'before the St Katherine Queen'. St Catherine was 'painted' here, presumably on the wall of this chapel, described as being quite small. Probably, the Wigley memorial, now high on the north wall of the chancel near the altar came from this chantry.

The Gell Chantry is in the north choir aisle and contains the Gell tombs and monuments. Of these the most important is the tomb of Anthony Gell of 1583, founder of Anthony Gell School and the Almshouses on the south side of the churchyard. It is not known to which saint the chantry was dedicated.

Outlying hamlets had parts of the church set aside for the use of those parishioners. The Alton Quire, the chapel for Alton and Idridgehay, appears to have been in St Edmund's chapel, an area used, certainly in 1710 when Francis Bessano visited and recorded it, as the Vestry. The chapel for Callow, appears to have been in the south transept, the opposite and partner to the Alton Quire, but had lost all its monuments by 1710. The Ible chantry or chapel was in north nave aisle. Unknown now, but recorded in 1710, as being 'founded by the Lords of Ible', for some time the Sacheverells later the Stathams. Like the Callow chapel it had lost all its monuments by 1710, felt to be due to defacement in the Civil War.

Two further chantries existed, St Helen's Chantry founded in 1505 by Richard Smyth, vicar since 1487 and St Mary's Chantry, apparently founded by the Lowes. A monument to the Lowes is on the north Chancel apse wall, which cannot be its original position.

The medieval church, whose interior largely remained when Francis Bassano saw it in 1710, then suffered a series of restorations and repairs some of which did damage rather than anything else. The first of these in 1724 was not particularly injurious, but in 1820 the most appalling damage was done in a shambolic 'restoration' described as barbarous very soon afterwards. Little better was done again in 1855. It was not until work by Sir Gilbert Scott in 1870 that serious attempts were made to undo the wretchedness of the 1820 work. This resulted in the interior of the church being restored to a little of its medieval glory, although the roof was raised to a higher pitch over the nave at the same time and this gave the exterior a rather lumpen appearance, which can be seen in Victorian pictures and drawings of the church. Finally, this misjudgment itself was addressed in 1926 when the nave roof was lowered and restored to the delicate proportions of the Perpendicular style of the 1500s, which best suit it. It is now after all its trials and tribulations a fine building in a peaceful, cathedral-like churchyard.

The Growth of the Town from the Medieval Period

The development of medieval Wirksworth as a prosperous town, based on its lead industry, is often commented upon, but this has never really been quantified. To understand the importance of Wirksworth in the medieval period suitable comparisons with other places need to be developed. This is not an easy task for comparative figures are difficult to find. However, there are Minister's Accounts for Wirksworth; these are the accounts of the manor, compiled annually by the Bailiff. A vast number of these accounts survive for Wirksworth in the National Archives at Kew.

From these accounts and other sources we know that by the 13th century Wirksworth had three manors. The major manor was the royal or Duchy of Lancaster manor as has been outlined earlier. This royal manor seems to have been divided during this time creating a second manor, sometimes known as the Holland, Exeter or Richmond Manor. This was probably a gift of part of the Lancaster holding to a trusted Duchy servant John de Holland who was created Duke of Exeter in 1397 by his half-brother King Richard II. The Holland family had risen to fame and fortune as officials for the Duchy of Lancaster during the early medieval period and Henry, the younger son of John de Holland rose to rank of Duke of Exeter. In 1461 he followed the Lancastrian cause, his lands were forfeited and the Holland Manor reverted to the Crown. It passed to Anne, Duchess of Exeter, sister of the Yorkist King Edward IV. In later years this manor was sometimes known as the Richmond Manor. The Lancastrian John of Gaunt had been made Earl of Richmond in 1342 and this may be the source of the name.

Holland Manor House, China House Yard: A house that bears this name is in St. Mary's Gate adjacent to China House Yard, the site of the later Wirksworth China factory. It has a bay window facing west over St Mary's Gate and appears from the outside to have no great antiquity. A study of the 1709 map of the town centre by Samuel Hutchinson made for the estate of Sir Philip Gell does not show a significant house on this site. However the Holland Manor was granted to the Gells of Hopton in the 1560s and on the map this area is included.

Thirdly, Wirksworth had a rectorial manor, which comprised church lands whose purpose was the upkeep of the chancel of the church. The date of this, 1272, suggests it was another royal gift after Wirksworth was acquired by the king from Robert de Ferrers. This was in the hands of the Dean of Lincoln. A 19th century map shows these rectorial holdings. They included the land and buildings where the Town Hall and the Vicarage now stand, the west side of Church Street, part of the west side of St Mary's Gate and the whole of the block on the north side of the Market Place with, oddly, the Duchy Steward's House and the Red Lion. The south-east end of St John's Street from number 41 south to the Wheatsheaf was also included and one house in the Cock Pit, as well as some farmland. The rectory belonged to the Dean of Lincoln and tithes were payable to him. In 1310 his manor consisted of 60 acres of land and some tenants who paid suit to his court. It was a profitable living with various dues being paid. By Henry VIII's time a vicarage house and garden, Easter dues and tithes of lead, geese, pigs, eggs, hemp & flax totalled an income of £42 7s 9d each year. The Dean of Lincoln continued to hold manorial land and buildings in the town until well into the 20th century.

Accounts for the Royal Manor and its lands in 1314 comprised income from the following sources:
- rents from tenants of land, tofts and buildings
- income from court fines
- rent and profits from the mill
- rent of the fishery of the Ecclesbourne
- income from the market and fair, tolls and tallage (land tax)
- income from small sales of food grown and renting out of pasture
- with a total income for the year 1314-1315 a little over £90 at the time.

An account for the Holland Manor in 1280-1 shows it was both smaller and evidently less urban in its income, which included:
- rents from tenants
- income from court fines
- income from the sale of grain
- income from the sale of stock animals, chickens, cows etc
- with a total income for the year 1280-1281 a little over £44 at the time.

Given the difference in dates of these two accounts, these figures nevertheless suggest the Holland Manor was worth about half as much as the Duchy of Lancaster Manor. This being the case, the total income for the town's manors at the end of the 13th century might be argued to be of the order of £120. These accounts do not include any income from the sale of lead or the rectorial income. The value of each thirteenth dish of ore sold was given to the king and this was accounted for through Exchequer accounts separate from the manor.

This £120 manorial income can be compared with the income for other towns. For example there is a very extensive survey, the Kilwardby Survey, of the manors of the Archbishop of Canterbury for 1279. In this, the income for Croydon in that year was £80, for Wimbledon £66, for Aldington was £192 (the largest) and for Maidstone was £86. These comparisons are perhaps straws in the wind, as land use and circumstances differ, but, overall, Wirksworth rests in the top quarter of income when compared to the 24 locations listed in the Kilwardby survey, and this sets aside Wirksworth's income from the lead industry and whatever the rectorial manor generated for the church. In short, Wirksworth was a rich manor.

The Manor Courts

Each of the three manors in Wirksworth, the royal manor, the Holland manor and the rectorial manor operated their own manorial courts and many of the records for these courts exist in the Derbyshire and other record offices. The records of the Wirksworth manor courts are very extensive and a huge resource yet to be seriously investigated. The record of the royal and Holland manors tend to get mixed up as they are often just headed 'Wirksworth' in catalogues, although those for the rectorial manor (the Dean of Lincoln's manor) are usually more clearly catalogued.

Manor courts had two components: a Court Baron to deal with issues related to manorial tenants and their tenancies and a Court Leet to deal with lower issues. These included enquiring regularly into the condition of watercourses, roads, paths, and ditches; guarding against all manner of encroachments on public rights; preserving landmarks; keeping watch and ward in the town; overlooking the common lands, the rights over them and restraining cases of excessive use by the pasturing animals; guarding against the adulteration of food; inspecting weights and measures; looking in general at the morals of the people and finding remedies for social ills and inconveniences. It also had to address the grosser crimes such as assault, arson, burglary, murder, treason and other felonies. For example, this action was brought to the Wirksworth Court Leet in November 1558, when the wretched and bellicose John Wigley was accused of blocking the Hopton Road (Hopton Lane). This was one of several court cases involving Wigley – he was a serial offender, even his family are known to have taken him to court.

The Court Leet of Wirksworth November 1558

'The jurie appointed doo present that John Wigley of Wirkesworthe hathe set one wall up on a place nere Wirkesworthe called Yokkyffe whiche wall thereof is set and yet standeth in the Quenes highewaye leadynge between the towne of Wirkesworthe and Hopton[1] and the jurie also doo present that by reason of the said wall so sett & standinge the highewaye is turned upon the inheritance of Anthony Gell and therefore they sett a payne[2] that the said John Wigley doo remove the said wall so yet the common highewaye may have its right course, on thisyde the next Lete upon payne of himself'.

[1]Ashbourne had been originally written but was crossed out, because the Queen's Highway to Ashbourne was the road from Wirksworth via Kirk Ireton and Bradley.
[2]make an order usually with a fine if it is not carried out.

We have no way of knowing whether the Court was successful in having Wigley's wall removed from the road and its rightful course restored, instead of running over Anthony Gell's inheritance (his land). The modern cramped and winding course of Hopton Lane as it lies beside Bowsfield does not visually give the impression of being wholly correct, so maybe his wall remained in place.

Over time the activities of the Court Leet were overtaken by changes in the manor, court and county council system. Most Courts Leet were finally abolished under the Administration of Justice Act 1977.

The Market Place and its Surroundings

Around the churchyard market stalls and booths would have been set up from very early times and fairs were held there on feast days. Although the market charter was only issued in 1306 it is certain that a market operated in Wirksworth before the end of the 13th century, as can be seen from Edmund's 1296 Inquisition

Wirksworth, Old Market Place

post mortem quoted earlier. As a royal manor it was possibly not deemed necessary to have a charter for the holding of a market, but with the changing of manorial ownership in the thirteenth century a regularisation of the situation took place and a charter issued in 1306. This granted the right to hold a market on Tuesdays and a fair annually for three days in September at the Nativity of the Virgin, September 7-9th. Another fair is listed in a document from 1649 at the Feast of Philip and James on May 3rd.

The market place covered a much larger area than the present day site. It included the triangular area entered by Dale End and Coldwell Street at its NW and NE corners respectively and narrowing down to the south towards the present zebra crossing. The Swine Market was up West End with houses encroached onto it now making the road narrow. The block including the Hope and Anchor pub seems to be a further encroachment and another block of buildings above this are shown on an 18th century map and early 20th photographs. Sometime after 1925 these were demolished making the Market Place as it is today. Further forward encroachments onto the Market Place may have taken place on the west, north and east sides, making its area much smaller. A market cross stood in the market area in front of what is now Paynes the chemists and is marked on a map from 1709. It is possible that the piece of surviving knot-work built into the exterior north choir aisle wall of the church may be from this cross.

A Moot (or Market) Hall was a meeting place where local issues were dealt with and trading standards were overseen. The Barmote Court held here had its origins to the Burg Moots of the other Mercian chief towns and a consideration of their activities can illuminate us as to what the Wirksworth Court did in antiquity. In Canterbury the Court was engaged in the management of the town's trade and in its civic affairs; in Winchester the Court records its supervision of the night watch. An early reference to the building of a court house in Wirksworth was in 1474 when it was ordered that 80 oak trees be delivered from Shining Cliff woods for the building of a Moot Hall. On the earliest maps it is sited in the middle of the old Market Place where Harrison Drive has been cut through. Although described as being in great decay and in need of repairs in 1608, in 1649 it was described in a survey as *'A certaine place built of tymber and commonly called the Kings Moothall conteyning three bayes of building under which court room are built six butchers shops on the west side'*. It was rebuilt in the Market Place in 1773 by order of the Duchy of Lancaster. However they ordered its demolition in 1814 'due to the rowdy behavior and congestion by miners', but also possibly the building had been undermined. It was rebuilt on Chapel Lane and is where the Barmote Court meets each April. For almost 500 years a dish for measuring lead was kept here but in 2011 it was removed to Chatsworth by the Barmaster.

Around the churchyard and Market Place the houses of those living in the town would have clustered. Many of these parts of the historic centre of Wirksworth were composed of blocks of buildings. There was also clearly some encroachment development on the east side of the Market Place on what must originally have been the boundary of the churchyard and it is known that the churchyard was once larger than it now is. The market at Wirksworth was a key reason for the success of the town and a contributor to its prosperity. Here the stalls were set up in the early morning and crowds gathered for the opening of the market. The market bell opened the day and the shutters came down. Hundreds came to Wirksworth's market and by a small miracle in the modern world it still hangs on: long may it be before the market bell rings for the last time in the town.

Medieval Streets and Burgage Plots

St John's Street is unusual amongst the Wirksworth streets, in that it is relatively straight and wide and it has a certain dignity to it. In measuring the features of the street archaeologists found it to be exactly three perches wide and many of the house frontages a perch wide. A perch is a medieval unit of measurement, about five metres. Burgages were a medieval town planning activity, because creating them was a mechanism to improve the commercial attractiveness of a town. Space at the front was at a premium, plots are long and narrow, with a row of outbuildings stretching to the rear of the house or shop. They were rented in medieval times to merchants, tradesmen or shopkeepers and are known as burgage plots. Narrow plots of this type can be seen fronting St. John's Street. In addition, archaeologists working here in June 2015 began to discover large amounts of medieval pottery, dating from the eleventh century onwards. This discovery led to a re-assessment of the under-examined issue of burgage in Wirksworth.

There is a single documentary reference to a burgage plot in Wirksworth. A grant from Thomas le Daneys of various burgages and lands to Tutbury Priory, included a burgage in Tutbury, and one in Wirksworth. The grant has no date but refers to both William, Earl of Ferrers and his brother Robert, which gives a time frame for the grant of between 1261 when William came of age and 1269 when Robert lost

Artist's impression of the cruck cottage at the corner of St. Mary's Gate

his lands to royal control. It also states that these properties were formerly held by Brun de Colonia of *Echam*, possibly Oakham, suggesting that the burgage existed before the time frame of the grant. In Leeds the area of Burmantofts was an additional allocation of agricultural land given with burgages. This might be similarly true in Wirksworth; some local field names could be considered in the same light, particularly Burley Flatt, which contains the *bur* or *burgh* element.

Many of the houses in Wirksworth are older than their frontages suggest, for example numbers 15 and 17 St John's Street were the subject of dendrochronology dating (tree ring analysis) by Nottingham University which found them to have beams from trees felled in 1676. Given what is now known about the burgages, these houses are likely to be on plots or previous house sites which are much older. Possibly parts of North End and West End show the characteristics of this kind of burgage development too.

Archaeology lends a hand too as pottery found in St John's Street dates from the 11th century onward and this might imply early burgage development. The earliest pottery, Doncaster Frenchgate Ware, is from a time frame not before 1050 and unlikely to be after 1200, though pottery persists after the date of its making. As the de Ferrers were granted a market in Tutbury in 1086 and burgage is mentioned in Tutbury from 1141, we are probably seeing the same kind of commercial development activity by them in both Tutbury and Wirksworth at the same time. It was a way of improving their towns and consequently their assets and their income. In short, the Wirksworth burgage development may date from almost immediately after the Norman Conquest. What has not yet been solved is that although this development has all the characteristics of burgage plots, there is no evidence of the burgesses, it is not clear why this is, although the term 'Free Tenants' in the 1314 accounts might imply inhabitants of this status.

Mills

Every manor had a corn mill where the tenants had to have their corn ground and the first mill sites were water powered. On the earliest surviving map of Wirksworth, drawn in 1709, three mills and their dams are shown – one at Millers Green, known as Milnhouses in 1307, on a tributary of the Ecclesbourne river coming down from Callow; one on the Ecclesbourne itself on Water Lane; and a third at the site on Derby Road that is now Haarlem Mill.

The early reference to Millhouses suggests this site was that of the manorial corn mill from the medieval period. Speedwell Mill now stands here and was converted to a cotton mill by John Dalley by 1790 or 1791. By 1808 it had fallen into disuse and was converted to houses, later to become a hat factory and corn depot. Joseph Wheatcroft established a tape manufactory here in 1844.

The Water Lane Mill was called *Middle Miln* on the 1709 map. In the 17th and 18th centuries lead smelting took place here, a purpose that could have started in the medieval period. By 1816 a tape mill, Willow Bath Tape Mill, was operating on a site slightly to the north with a steam engine to power it. The mill that remains today has a chimney dated 1864 and till recently belonged to the Wirksworth Weaving Company.

The earlier name '*Middle Miln*' suggests another mill was sited somewhere else upstream from this site. The most likely site for the 'upper mill' was in the vicinity of New Bridge (Wash Green Bridge). Which of these sites is the manorial corn mill is difficult to judge and it is possible there were two corn mills in the town to serve the sizeable population and the two manors.

The site at Haarlem Mill on Derby Road was named as 'Walk Mill' on the 1709 map. Throughout the 15th and 16th centuries this is documented as *Walkmylne*. It is probably the site of the fulling mill described in the 1296 Inquisition post mortem. The name comes from the early process of 'walking' woollen cloth in a trough to clean and soften it, hence the surnames Walker and Fuller. Afterwards it was laid on 'tenters' or frames to stretch and dry it again, giving the field name Tenter Yard. Later history of this mill site suggests it was used for corn milling in the 1770s. In 1777 Sir Richard Arkwright bought the site from Philip Gell of Hopton and built a cotton spinning mill here. It was converted to tape weaving between 1813 and 1815 by Maddley, Hackett and Riley of Derby and they gave it the name Haarlem Mill. At some time silk was spun in part of the premises. About 1841 James and William Tatlow took over the mill. In 1792 it had a steam engine to fill the mill pond to maintain the water level to power the mill. This was housed in the engine shed abutting the south front. The long brick range on the west was built and reconstructed at different stages between about 1832 and 1885.

A 'new mill' is documented in a rental from 1473 next to Bowsfield. On the 19th century tithe map this field is shown on Hopton Lane above Yoke Cliff so the new mill was probably a windmill, a technology brought to England in the 12th century. It continued to grind corn until about 1830 and is the origin of the name of Windmill Farm on Hopton Lane.

Component Settlements

Steeple Grange

Land in this area to the north of the town was granted to Bicester Abbey in 1405 by two Wirksworth men, John Marchaunt and Marragdus Shorthose. It remained with the Abbey as an outlying grange or farm until the dissolution of the monasteries in 1538 when it was acquired by the Duke of Suffolk, then bought by the Blackwell family and later the Greensmiths. Steeple Hall, the former grange, was finally bought by Richard Arkwright from the Greensmiths in 1771. He demolished it and used the stone to build the first Cromford Mill. The road from Wirksworth to Cromford had followed the route of Old Lane but was altered in 1756 when the route was turnpiked. In 1836 the hamlet consisted of only 8 houses and still remained quite separate from the rest of the town until the growth of both brought the parts together.

Wash Green

First documented on a Duchy of Lancaster rental in 1415, this area may derive its name from the fact that lead ore was washed and cleaned here. Good water sources exist higher up the hill to the east which would have facilitated these processes. In 1827 there was a small tape mill, a sawmill, a bleach and dye works and a brick works in this area, quite a concentration of labour intensive industry.

Up the hill the House of Correction (town prison) was built in 1791 and later described in detail. *'At the back of the keepers house are two court yards, one for men the other for women about 28 feet by 19 feet 6 inches with a sewer in each. Nine steps down in the women's court is a damp dungeon, 7'6" by 6'4" high to the crown of the arch. All the light or ventilation here received through a grating in the door, 6" square. On each side of the keeper's apartment a door opens into a little day-room, 11'9" by 7' with a fireplace in both. These are for men and women and each has attached to it two small sleeping cells, 7'5" by 5'6" and 8' high, ventilated and lighted by a grating over each door... Wooden bedsteads only are provided by the county, straw in sacking and chaff beds are furnished by the keeper...there is no water but what is fetched from a distance'.* In 1805, J. Neild reported that there was only one prisoner, a shoemaker, who had been locked up for 'bastardy'. It was closed in 1827 when the new county gaol was opened in Derby.

Gorsey Bank

Another area of small cottages, possibly encroached on the 'wastes and commons' on the outskirts of the town. It remained quite separate from the rest of the town until the building of the local authority housing in the mid 20th century. Some of the cottages may have been to house workers at Providence Mill after it had been built by George Gamble in 1881. This was a tape mill, Wirksworth being famous for its red tape, but replaced an earlier saw mill.

The Dale and Greenhill and later encroachments on the 'wastes and commons'

In the medieval period the town would have been surrounded by farmland, much of which was unsuitable for growing crops. This rough grazing was often known as 'waste and commons' and was used by all for grazing animals. The hilly nature of the landscape close to the centre of town meant this waste ground could be 'encroached' for building as the town expanded in the late sixteenth and seventeenth centuries. It led to a piecemeal growth of small plots very evident up the Dale, on Greenhill, at Gorsey Bank and around Wash Green. These areas are often known as 'squatter settlements' as the people living there were outside the manorial system. A valuation in 1649 to regularise the situation of these cottagers shows their rents ranged from 4 pence to as much as 7 shillings, indicating a wide variety in quality and size. This 17th century development took place in a haphazard way, with cottages in small irregular plots traversed by short lanes creating a distinctive pattern. Between the Dale and Greenhill this area is known today as 'the Puzzle Gardens'. Other areas of encroachments are at Warmbrook and the Cock Pit just beyond the limits of the medieval town at the junction of three roads. In 1649 there were 4 cottages paying rent and 2 encroachments at Warmbrook. Similar development took place on Gorsey Bank and possibly up West End on the sides of the road making it the narrow way into town it is today.

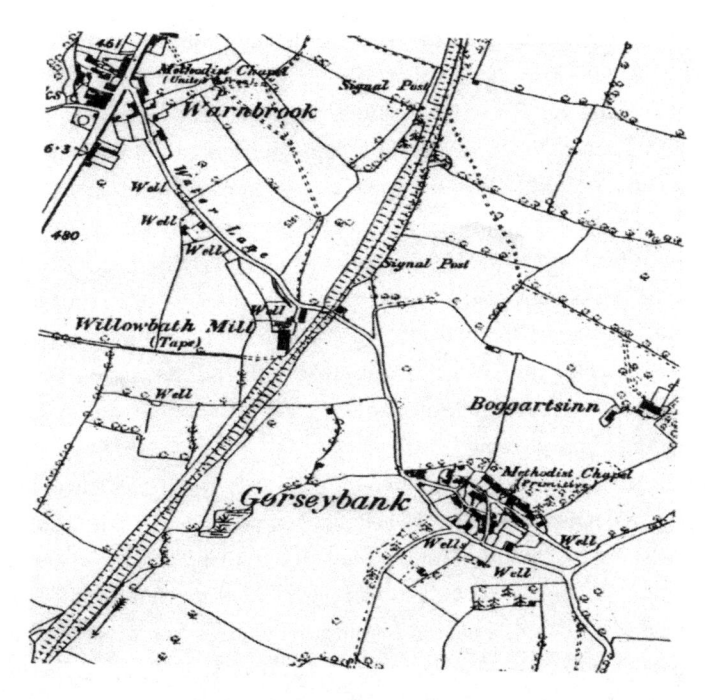

Map 5: Gorsey Bank in 1879

Bole Hill

Documentary evidence for this settlement on the hillside above Wirksworth dates from 1599 but it is likely it was here some time before that. The names derives from a 'bole' or lead smelting hearth, probably situated on the hill above the houses where the prevailing westerly winds would provide a good draft for smelting. An area of small cottages and four pubs in the 19th century (The Miner's Standard, New Inn, Hollybush and Railway Inn) it has its own distinct character. The cottages cluster around the Green and the Lanes and lead mine sites are still evident in the area. Other later industry in this area included gingham weaving workshops at Oaker House, cotton frame knitting in Hallams yard and a brickworks close to Black Rocks. The road going through Little Bolehill to the Malt Shovel pub was subject to a major land slip in 1979 and has been closed to traffic ever since.

Who Lived in Wirksworth?

Documents survive that give the names of tenants and landholders who lived in Wirksworth at the time the rental or survey was drawn up. They give snapshots of the people living in the town at the time, but not a full picture. All towns had a number of tradesmen, tailors, carpenters, stone masons and in Wirksworth's case lead miners and 'bolers'. All these appear as surnames in the rentals as do others that show where people originated from or where they were living.

The Lay Subsidy Roll of 1327-8 is the earliest surviving example of such a document for Wirksworth. King Edward III raised a tax to help fight a war with Scotland and all those with moveable items worth over 5 shillings were to give a twentieth of the value to the king. The section of the roll for the Wirksworth has not completely survived but 16 names appear together with the value of their goods and the amount of tax payable.

The major landowner in the town in the 15th century was the Duchy of Lancaster and a copy of a detailed rental survives in the National Archives from 1415. From this 57 names of people renting houses, cottages and land are documented, some with only a small amount of rent to pay each year, others much more. Many of these people held different parcels of land on different tenures. Some were free tenants, some tenants at will or by warranty, others in bondage usually called villeins. Among these tenants were William Sadler, Henry & William Taillour, Richard Smyth, Robert Barker (a leatherworker) and John Potts, all of whose names suggest

Wyrksworth	[Value]	[Tax]	Roger del Hay	45s	2s 3d
Nicolas Bate	35s	21d	Simon Hutte	15s	9d
William de Bradburn	55s	2s 9d	Nicholas de Midleton	60s	3s
Robert Bythebroc	50s	3s	Henry de Milnehouse	20s	12d
William Bythebroc	20s	12d	Peter de Stepul	41s 8d	2s 1d
Alex Carpenter	15s	9d	John Truselove	20s	12d
Cecilia widow of William de Carsington	50s	2s 6d	Nicholas Truslove	40s	2s
Thomas de Cromford	£7	7s	Randulf Tubret	25s	15d
Richard del Hay	31s 8d	19d	Summa bonorum	£33 13s 4d	33s 8d

The Lay Subsidy Roll of 1327-8 (spelling and sums modernised)

trades their families were engaged in. Others came from around the district, William Beighton, Robert Brookwallhurst, Nicholas Ibull and William Wynfeld for example. The property they were renting is interesting too as this is often the first occurrence in writing of the names of many of the places around the town still known today. Yokecliff was '*Zelcliff*', Pitty Wood was '*Pithey*', Warmbrook, Dale yard, Brokenstone Dale, Hollyn wall and Bradston are all there. No shops are mentioned, but there were forges, a kiln, a watermill and fishing in the Ecclesbourne, with many small parcels of land, an acre or two scattered in various fields around the town.

A typical entry reads '*Richard & Michael Harpour hold in bondage 3 acres in le Mylnehous feld, a house there, 2 acres on Coldbrokflatt, 2 acres on Hathurege cliff, 2 acres there, 1½ acres under le Holyn, ½ acre at le Fouldfeld, 1 acre next to Fouleside, 1 acre on Oldcroft, ½ acre at Ludwallhede, ½ acre next to Cresbroke, 1 acre at Crymbaulls, 1½ acre & 1 rod at Smythrudding, 1 garden called Wilezerd next to le Grene, 2 acres at Lightehulle, ½ acre there & 2 acres in Smythrudding*'.

Two further fifteenth century rentals of premises and land also furnish us with names of the tenants of the Holland manor within the parish, one for John de Holand in 1420-1 and another for 1473 for Anne Duchess of Exeter, of the same manor. In 1420 surnames similar to those above occur: William Taylor held some land, 2 gardens and part of the Hannage, John Webster had land at Oathill, Robert Odyngham held land '*under the Porteway in the Dale*', Thomas the Glover held a close called *Gylkhill* (the Gilkin), John Walker had *Pittay* (Pittywood) and more besides, William Wright held 3 cottages and other land, William Broklehurst, William Winfield and numerous others with small parcels of land spread throughout the area. Other tenants and under-tenants are detailed with the land, cottages, barns and gardens they rented.

In 1473 John Fletcher had 2 acres on Oathill, John Robyson, a tailor, had land in the *Hennege* (The Hannages), Richard Blackwall meadow in *Whassemeydow* (Wash Meadow), Henry Stone has a place called *Stadfall* and Richard Spenser has the Bowfields. Cottages and gardens, a tenter yard (a place for drying and stretching woollen cloth), a new mill and a cemetery are also recorded.

Anthony Gell Grammar School

The first reference to a school in Wirksworth comes in the will of Agnes Fearne, the daughter of Ralph Gell. The Gell family were establishing themselves as local landowners and minor gentry from the early 16th century, having made money from their interest in the lead industry. From 1553 Ralph Gell leased the Holland manor in Wirksworth and after his death in 1564 his numerous children, notably Anthony, Thomas and John continued to influence town life. In 1574 Agnes Fearne left 5 marks a year 'to the use of and maintaining of the free school in Wirksworth' if 'after my decease there shall happen to be any free school within the town'. When Anthony died in 1583 his will, which had been made in 1578 and signed in February 1579, stipulated that his brother Thomas should 'obtain a licence for erecting a free school' and he listed parcels of land the rent from which was to maintain the school. These included a 'schoolhouse which I lately builded'. The Charter for Anthony Gell's Grammar School was granted by Queen Elizabeth I on 27th of October 1583. The provision of a school in the town appeared to stimulate others to follow, Ashbourne in 1585, Chesterfield in 1598 and Bakewell, rather tardily, in 1637.

The original Grammar School was probably built on the site to the east of the churchyard where the building called Old Grammar School now stands. This particular building was designed and built by William Maskrey, the Wirksworth stonemason in 1828, replacing an earlier one described as being 'in a ruinous state'. It continued in use together with the new buildings built on the Hannages in 1907. These were designed by the county architect George Widdows, where Anthony Gell School remains to this day.

The Almshouses

Anthony Gell also willed that his executor Thomas 'within a year and a half of my death shall bestow of the making and building of one almshouse in the side of the Hannage near the new bridge the sum of £60.' During the next ten years after his death 'six aged, poor and impotent men' were to be placed in the almshouses and given £20 between them during these ten years. Both Anthony and Francis Bunting gave £5 per annum towards the expenses of the men and sixpence a week in bread. Built at the end of the 16th century by the side of the churchyard, rather than a site closer to the New Bridge, the almshouses are still occupied today and run by the Anthony Gell and Anthony Bunting Almshouses Charitable Trust. Others, including a Robert Sage in 1661, contributed both to the school, the poor and the almshouses.

Stuart Expansion

By the 17th century the survival of documents increases. In 1627 King Charles I levied a tax on his subjects known as 'An Ayd to His Majesty King Charles', under the guise of 'a loan'. From this we know the names of those living in Wirksworth at that time who were considered rich enough to pay – nine names appear: Richard Wigley, John Topleis, Robert Feilding, Richard Lee, Thomas Taylor, George Somers, Dionise Wetton, John Ormefield and Henry Buxton.

A more detailed document survives from 1649 at the time of the Commonwealth when Parliament ordered a valuation of royal property before a possible sale. They wanted to know what rents and dues were owed to them. A number of these Parliamentary Commissions were instigated and one such for Wirksworth gives us a lot of detail about who was living in the town at this time. The various categories of tenants are listed starting with those living on 'the wastes' of the manor. These are in effect squatters who have taken advantage of a common belief that if a house was erected on the common land in a manor overnight they then had the right of undisturbed possession. To make things more difficult for squatters the Erection of Cottages Act was passed in 1588 whereby a cottage could only be built if it had a minimum of 4 acres associated with it. This rental puts value on these 'encroached' cottages no doubt with a view to them becoming rentable at a later date. These cottages are found at Newbridge, upon Greenhill, in the Dale, at Warmbrook and at *Longoe bank,* thirty in total. A smithy at Bayley Croft and a cowhouse at North Town End were also listed. The next category are those living in properties owned by the manor and leased 'for a term of years', leaseholders. This includes further cottages but also the lease of the Fairs and Market, a smithy, 2 coal pits on Longway Bank, the Moothall, shops, a barn and 8 acres of coppice and shrub at Waterdale Shrugges, land overlooking Water Lane. Following this are lists of freeholders, 36 names in total with rents from 2d to 11s 8d, copyholders with agreed rents, 54 names with similar rental amounts, and 22 copyholders who had not yet made such agreements. The whole was overseen by Abell Richardson, George Southcotte, John Thorne, William Tracy and William Webb, the Supervisor General.

The Hearth Tax Return of 1670 gives details of houses with a number of hearths that could be taxed. For Wirksworth 135 houses had one hearth, 56 houses had two, 19 had three, 12 had four, 5 had five, 5 had six and three houses belonging to Edward Milward, Mr. Ballcoose and Mr. Browne respectively had eight each. Only two houses are identified by name: Steeple House which had just one hearth and The Gate House that had six hearths.

From this period of Wirksworth's history many houses and features still survive. Discussion on these is found below. The closeness of the dating of these important 17th century houses would suggest that at this time Wirksworth was enjoying a period of sufficient prosperity that a major rebuilding was being undertaken in and around the town, stimulated by the activities of lead merchants and the profitability of lead during the 30 years war. The medieval style of building was to use a timber-frame infilled with lime plaster and rubble panels. One of these timber 'cruck' or crooked frames was revealed in a cottage on the corner of St. Mary's Gate and has been left exposed to view. Other timber frames are still hidden within existing buildings. The rebuilding was in stone, still a novelty in 1606 as one house is referred to as *'messuage called the Stone House'*. This rebuilding continued throughout the seventeenth century, with a gap during the English Civil war. Even lesser houses were rebuilt as has been seen in St John's Street.

The Old Manor House and the demolished Wirksworth Hall

A house now known as the Old Manor House is on Coldwell Street. It stands on a large plot of land with a walled garden and was once called 'The Gables'. This is basically an early 17th century house with three gabled bays and mullioned windows and 18th century additions. We know from the 1296 Inquisition post mortem of Edmund Earl of Lancaster that there was a 'capital messuage' in Wirksworth, often known as a Hall or Manor House but whether it was on this site is not known. The Lancasters were not resident in the town but may have visited and a steward possibly lived here.

There was a *Halle Orchard* recorded in 1415 suggesting that an earlier house of some size was in existence at that time, but the reference gives no location for the Orchard so we cannot know, whether the Old Manor House represented this early Hall or it was on the site of the demolished Wirksworth Hall. This stood on the other side of Coldwell Street where Hall Gardens now are. Built by the Hurt family of Alderwasley in 1779, some sources indicate this was a rebuilding of a previous house. The Hurts were landowners and lead merchants and the Hall was demolished in 1922 due to subsidence. The stable block for this is in Blind Lane and the stable block and the building now known as The Old Manse are the only standing reminders of the former Hall. The fine wrought iron screen gates once at the entrance to Wirksworth Hall were removed after the Hall was demolished and now stand at Henley Hall near Ludlow.

Hopkinson's House, 1-3 Greenhill

This is a large early seventeenth century house built in limestone with gritstone quoins, lintels and mullions. A piece of moulded plasterwork from a chimney-breast was rescued after the roof collapsed in 1954 and bears the date 1631. The four bays along the frontage give it a distinctive roofline. It was built by William Hopkinson out of the profits of the lead industry and the probate inventory for Anne Hopkinson, his mother, in 1648 gives the contents of named rooms and outbuild-

Wirksworth Hall in 1920, two years before its demolition.

ings: the great chamber, the chamber over the parlour, the chamber over the buttery, the white chamber, the study chamber, the entry chamber, the brewhouse chamber, the corn chamber, the buttery, the dining parlour, the hall, the nether parlour, the kitchen, the larder, the milkhouse, the brewhouse, the hen house and the stable chamber. Anne left the house to her offspring and over the years it was divided amongst them eventually becoming one dwelling again in the early 18th century when a John Toplis of Brookwalls was in possession of it. Until the beginning of the 20th century the upper floor had been used as a bakery. It had got into a parlous state of repair before the Civic Trust's Wirksworth Project in the 1970s when it was restored primarily for office use.

Babington House, Greenhill

The only house of any size on Greenhill was probably built around 1630 in coursed limestone rubble with gritstone quoins, lintels and mullions. It has two storeys and attics, a stone slate roof and gritstone ridge tiles. In the garden behind the house is an appreciable quarried rock face. Geological research, using microfossils, has indicated that the highest beds in the quarry can be correlated with the lowest courses of limestone in the house. As one moves down the quarry so the building rose. In short, the house was built from its own quarry. Supposedly it has associations with Anthony Babington of Dethick who plotted to rescue the imprisoned Mary Queen of Scots. No evidence has been found to substantiate this link and, as he died in 1586, it is unlikely the house was built by him. No Babingtons are listed in 1670 Hearth Tax return. It is called Greenhill House on the 1st edition of the OS map. Between 1724 and 1829 it was used as a Poor House (workhouse) and then from 1867 to 1928 as a Cottage Hospital. Its role as a Poor House was recorded in 1797:

> 'The Workhouse is an old building, not originally intended for the purpose; it is not in a good situation, but as far as its construction will permit, kept clean and airy. The following is the weekly diet: Breakfast—Sunday, Wednesday, Friday—bread and broth, rest of the week—milk pottage; Dinner—Sunday, Wednesday, Friday—bread, broth, butcher's meat, potatoes, etc., Monday—baked puddings and treacle sauce, Tuesday, Thursday, Saturday—Bread and milk; Supper—milk pottage and bread every day. On meat days the proportion is at 20 lbs. meat for 30 persons. The children are kept very clean, and are instructed in their catechism, reading, etc. Few of the inmates are able to work, those who are spin lint, tow, etc., for the use of the house. They are allowed

one penny for every 7d. of spinning. The rooms are of various sizes and contain 2 to 7 beds each. The beds and pillows are filled with chaff and have 2 sheets, 1 blanket and 1 coverlet. There are at present 28 persons in the house, 12 under 7 years of age. Subscriptions for the Poor last winter [1794-5] amounted to £60, which were laid out in purchasing coal, beef, and potatoes. The Poor in the Workhouse have oat bread, but no beer or cheese, except at Christmas. A sort of gruel called water pottage, consisting of a small proportion of oatmeal and a small onion boiled with water, was eaten with bread twice, and sometimes thrice a day, by many people in this neighbourhood. It was much used during the late hard season. The cost of such a meal was about 1¼d. for each adult. Several small donations, amounting to £45 10s, are distributed yearly among the Poor who do not receive any parish relief.'

The Old Manor House, Hopkinson's House and Babington House form a group, three of a kind; they all have a familiarity of architecture of the second quarter of the 17th century.

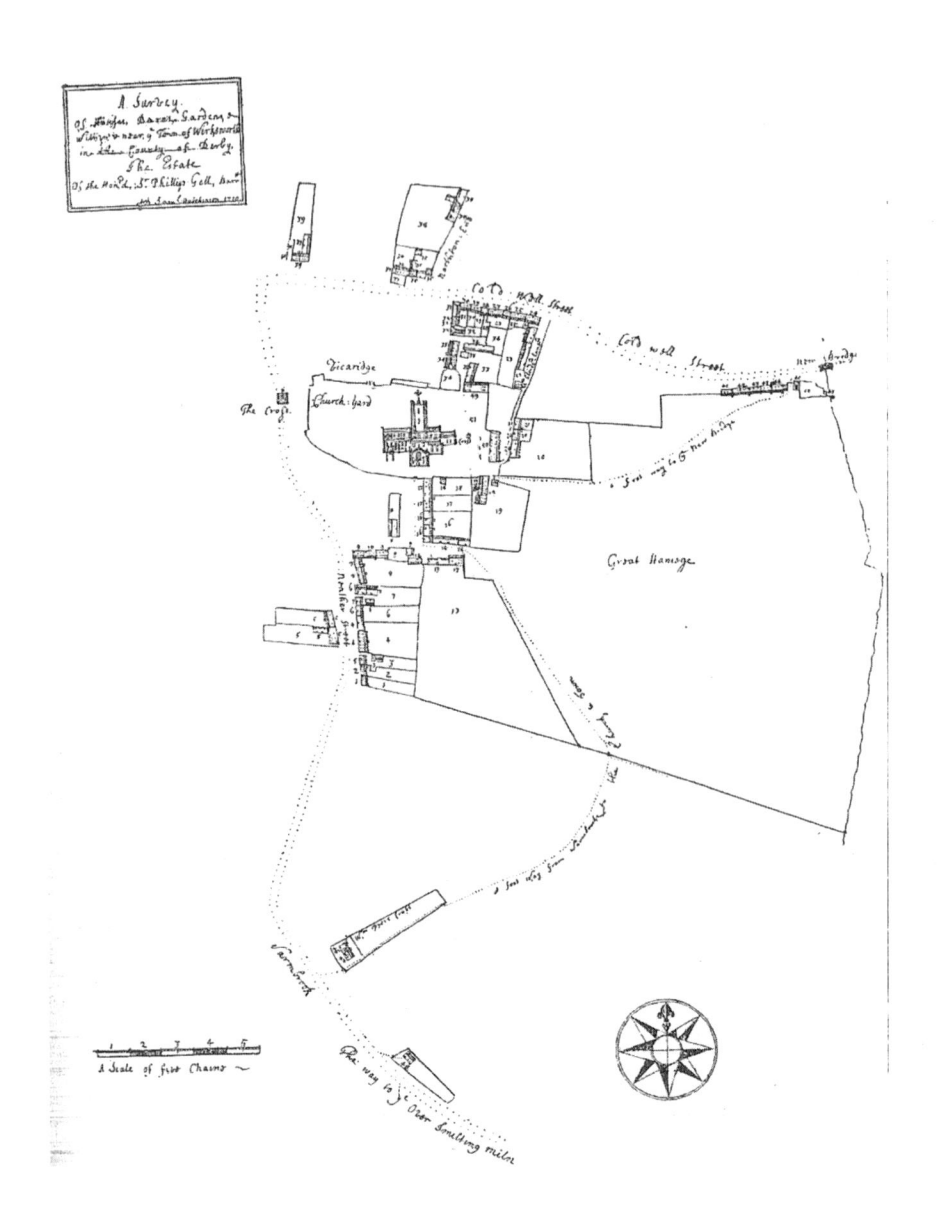

A Table wherein the figures
refer to ye Houses, Barns, Gardens &c

1. Widow Slackis a House & garden
2. Wid. Bolford House & garden
3. Wid. Archedinds House & garden
4. Jn° Hitloby's House, Barn, & garden
5. Wid. Wheatcroft, House, Barn & gardens
6. Rob.t Spaniors, House, Barn, Slaughterhouse
7. Wid. Poldoy's House, Barn, Smithy, & garden
8. Brabants Daughters House & garden
9. Edw. Wheatcroft two Houses, a workhouse &c
10. Edw. Burbury. a House
11. Ralph Brusil, a House & garden
12. Rob.t Thorpe a Barn
13. Harry Farrand, House, Barn, & garden
14. Elisha Hodgkinson. a Stable
15. m.r Ridgeway a Barn
16. Owen Ragg, two Houses & a garden
17. Jn° Ormsforde House & a garden
18. m.rs Alsop, a House & garden
19. Jn° Shadcroft. House Stable, Nerling grass
20. Jn° Pestr. House, & Garden, of Gregory, & Ho..
21. Eliz Guy's, House & garden
22. Wid Hawksham. a House & garden
23. Just Roalte House, Barn, & garden
24. Wid Wood. House & garden
25. Jn° Smith. a House & garden
26. Tho Blounts. House
27. Jn° Nailer. a House & garden.
28. Norman Stafford a House & garden.
29. Ann Ellin. House & garden
30. Sarah Toglor a House & garden
31. Jn° Blacknails. House & garden.
32. Wid Ellen & Barn. Smithy, & maltkiln
33. Tho Groasdall House, Barn, Bakehouse & garden
34. Tho Taylor. House, Barn & two gardens
35. Tho Collinson House, Stable, & garden.
36. Wid Buntinge, a House & garden.
37. Jn° Blount. House & garden
38. Adam Ragg, a House, Stable & garden
39. Will Poor, a House, Barn & garden
40. Philyp. Gell. a Gatehouse, Chamber &ar
41. Tho Malher. a House
42. James Malher a House.
43. Tho Poples. a House, Barn & Battery
44. Jn°. Gregory House Cow house & yard
45. Wid Bradshaw. a House
46. Wid. Molinus a House
47. Wid Malher a House
48. Fran.s Page a House & garden
49. The Free School
50. The Alms Houses
51. A piece of Land joyns to ye churchyard

Map 6: Survey of Sir Philip Gell's estate in Wirksworth 1710
(with accompanying list of properties shown on the map)

Chapter 3

1700 to the Present Day

Georgian Prosperity

IN 1725 DANIEL Defoe visited Wirksworth. He found it 'a large, well frequented market town ... the people generally coming twelve or fifteen miles to the market and sometimes much more; though there is no great trade to this town but what relates to the lead works, and to the subterranean wretches, who they call Peakrills, who work in the mines, and who live all round this town every way. The inhabitants are a rude, boorish kind of people, but they are bold, daring and even desperate kind of fellows in their search into the bowels of the earth, for no people in the world out-do them'.

Lead had been mined in the area at least since Roman times and Wirksworth's prosperity depended on it. The landscape to the north of the town is marked by disused lead workings and Bole Hill is a reminder of the earliest form of lead smelting. The lead mining area around Wirksworth is known as the King's Field because the Sovereign is entitled to a proportion of all lead that is mined. Since the 15th century the Crown sub-leased these royalties starting with a 40-year lease to the Earl of Warwick in 1468. Figures on lead output suggest there were peaks in production in the late 16th, late 17th and middle 18th centuries. After 1760 output fell but had occasional short-lived booms, the last being in the 1860's.

The town's prosperity at this time should not be under-estimated, within Derbyshire only Derby and Chesterfield were more affluent. Further rebuilding took place in the town. Until the 1750s much of the development might be described as being vernacular, that is the use of local materials by local craftsmen. Older style 17th century small mullion windows can be found in a number of cottages with later 'Georgian' windows and doors added. Some houses at the south end of St John's Street show the later 18th century rebuilding: numbers 40 and 42 were originally one house and, in particular, number 32 with its fine frontage and window pattern is entirely characteristic of its building date of 1750 and was also built on what had been two plots. Similar rebuilding took place in other parts of the town, some of which was in response to the opening of the 1756 turnpike road between Derby and Wirksworth, number 22 Wash Green being such an example. It was rebuilt in 1758 as the Ship Inn. The turnpike was known as 'top road' and led from the Moot Hall in the Market Place, along Coldwell Street, up Wash Green and to Derby via the Bear at Alderwasley to Belper Lane End and Duffield.

The town centre around Market Place was effectively redeveloped in a classical style. The number of permanent shops increased as their rather more affluent goods were more suited to the wider range of employed people than the lead miners, who tended to rely only on the market for essential foods and supplies. The impact of this was that the 'shopping centre' of Wirksworth was one of the top three in Derbyshire in the years between 1787 and 1828 even though, by the early 1800s Wirksworth's position was beginning to be eroded by rapid increases in the population of the nearby industrial town Belper to an estimated 4,500. Wirksworth's population was 3,474 in 1801. However, Belper largely relied on Wirksworth for its services, for despite its rapid increase in population, Belper in 1801 had little of the infrastructure of a town, no school, no House of Correction, no Poor House or bank and most of its supplies originated in Derby or Wirksworth.

The classical outlook of the Georgian Market Place arrived with the construction of a new Moot Hall in 1773 in a fine, metropolitan Palladian style, designed by Joseph Pickford. There followed a major rebuild of the frontage of the Red Lion in 1768 in a Palladian style and the extension to the Duchy Steward's House, with its Venetian windows, of about 1770.

Symond's House, 15 Market Place

This fine three-storied building on the Market Place was built for the Steward of the Duchy of Lancaster in 1753, panelling from that date survives inside as does a fine staircase window at the back. It has an enclosed garden behind with a mulberry tree. A later 'Palladian style' building was added in 1770, designed by the architect Joseph Pickford. Mr. Manlove, possibly Edward Manlove who was Steward of the Barmote Court in the mid 17th century, was charged for 6 hearths in the Hearth Tax of 1670 perhaps for an earlier house that stood on this site. Opposite, at Dale End, currently fronted by a bookshop, is the final piece of the classical jigsaw, a townhouse commissioned sometime just before 1774 by the Rev. Thomas Gell, now rather neglected and forgotten.

The culmination of this town centre development in the late eighteenth century gave Wirksworth a grandeur now lost. The 1773 Moot Hall was demolished a little after 1815 and replaced by the plain Moot Hall on Chapel Lane, a monument to the parsimony of the Duchy after the Napoleonic War. Various reasons are given for the premature demolition of the 1773 building, such as 'noisy miners' or 'an obstruction to traffic'. The Gell Archive at the Derbyshire Record Office makes it clear. It contains a rather bad-tempered letter of 1813 from the Duchy in London demanding that the town 'increase its subscription' to replace the 'dilapidated and dangerous' 1773 Moot Hall.

This period of prosperity saw Wirksworth reach the high point of its development with the lead industry sufficiently strong to remain important. Cotton spinning was developed in 1771 by Arkwright with his first mill at Cromford, increased the population in that village which was dependent on services in Wirksworth. Six years later Arkwright leased the Haarlem Mill site for the same purpose. He rebuilt the mill by 1780 and installed a reciprocating steam engine to refill the mill-dam with water. This powered the mill via the mill wheel from the Pittywood Stream. By 1789 the mill was employing 200 people.

From 1750 Wirksworth's peak of prosperity lasted over half a century. Its finest year in the opinion of Dr. Dack was 1780, a year she describes as Wirksworth's 'Annus Mirabilis': its miracle year. Not only had all these developments taken place but its services continued to expand and in that year John Toplis opened the first bank in Wirksworth, on St John's Street in the present Solicitors premises. This also resulted in the construction in 1782 of Nether House on the east side of St John's Street, with gardens behind, as the Toplis residence. This gave style to that street and the house was in later years described as the most dignified house in Wirksworth. On the opposite side of the road, Waltham House was

Lost buildings of Wirksworth
NETHER HOUSE
(1782-1935)

West Front (stone) Drawing by Anton Shone 2016

built in 1777 in much the same style. It was owned through the 19th century by the Wheatcroft family, owners of various of the tape mills.

The Gate House, the Causeway

A much earlier house must have stood on this site than the one that is there today. It is first documented in 1553 when John Wigley of the Gatehouse, Wirksworth married Helena Gell. Their son Francis who married Elizabeth Blackwall of Blackwall also lived there as did their son Thomas Wigley. In 1670 it had 6 hearths that were taxable. The present 3-storey red brick house of 3 bays was built by Philip Gell about 1770. At the rear of the present building a few 17th century mullioned windows can be seen with some other earlier stonework. At one time some members of the Arkwright family occupied it.

Hope and Anchor Public House

This large public house appears to be an encroachment onto the medieval market place. There are traces of 17th century stonework at the rear and to the side. The front is early 19th century with three storeys, sash windows and a cast-iron inn-sign. In the lounge bar there is a remarkable oak overmantel of crude execution and dated from around 1610. A first floor room has an enriched plaster ceiling as does the entrance lobby, from around 1630. A similar ceiling remains in the Old Manor House and all are similar to that in the Gatehouse Tower at Haddon Hall. It is possible a company of plasterers employed by the Manners family at Haddon also worked here in Wirksworth. The detailed history of this building is problematical and any 19th century writers' suggestions are best ignored.

Red Lion Hotel

This imposing building at the head of the old Market Place has all the look of an eighteenth century coaching inn. The arched entrance leads to a rear yard and an Assembly Room upstairs. A large chimney obvious from Harrison's Drive suggests a substantial fireplace from a much earlier medieval building is hidden inside. However there is no documented mention of the name before 1715. A survey for the billeting of soldiers in 1686 suggests Wirksworth had 80 guest beds and space for 266 horses in its inns, but sadly none of them were named.

On a 1709 map of Wirksworth showing properties which Philip Gell owned, this site has 'a gatehouse, chambers and garden', but no mention of an inn as such. By

1715 Gilbert Swift was the proprietor of the Red Lion. In his will he left a quantity of knives and forks, a coffee grinder and two violins.

The Red Lion was completely rebuilt by later owner Francis Hurt in 1768, with a Palladian windowed frontage and an Assembly Room on the first floor. This new frontage might represent a further encroachment onto the old Market Place. The Assembly Room helps illustrate the inn's importance to Wirksworth's social hierarchy. Assemblies or balls were held each year during this period, where the local gentry and their sons and daughters would meet. This also tells us that Wirksworth was an important town socially.

John Salt was the Innkeeper in Francis Hurt's time, continuing the assemblies and also promoting classical concerts in the Moot Hall. When Francis Hurt died in 1785 and John Salt retired, the assemblies were no longer held on a regular basis and the Red Lion settled down into its role as the chief amongst Wirksworth's three principal inns, with the Hope and Anchor and the Crown Inn (closed in 1910) being the others. At this time a cart ran from the Red Lion to Derby and back on Mondays and Fridays and the Excise Office operated from the Red Lion as well. Later innkeepers at the Red Lion are known to be Francis Walker in 1791, Samuel Harley in 1821, Benjamin White in 1835, Samuel Rowland in 1846, Henry Walker in 1861 and 1871, Thomas Baggaley in 1881, Edward Roobottom in 1891, George Glover in 1901, John Boam 1913, John Oates 1950, Peter Booth 2015 and others. It retains its Assembly Room, still used for functions, and a cantilevered stone staircase to the upper floors with its original iron railings, quite rare today.

Nineteenth Century Industry

Despite the earlier affluence the lead industry was only intermittently profitable at the end of the eighteenth century and the beginning of the nineteenth. Even with the employment generated by cotton spinning and textiles the prosperity of Wirksworth could not be sustained in the face of the industrial revolution taking place faster in other towns. The lack of expansion of other forms of employment in services, inn-keeping, shops and supplies and poor transport links did not help. Worse was to come. The lead industry was in terminal decline and the small textile and other industries had yet to take its place. Even so, in 1806 lead production was sufficiently important for Wirksworth to be described as lying 'in a bottom eternally overhung with smoke from the lead and calamine works, the principal covering being here and there broken into pillars of white smoke from smelting mills'.

However, once the demand for lead stimulated by the Napoleonic War was over and imported lead was being brought in more cheaply, the end could easily be seen. Wirksworth was less likely to be regarded as an important town and this was evident in road developments in the early years of the nineteenth century.

Wirksworth's road network, the life-blood of its commerce, was gradually bypassed by the building of new turnpike roads. In 1820 a road was opened up the Derwent Valley northwards from Belper via Cromford and Matlock in effect isolating Wirksworth and having the effect that Belper no longer relied on Wirksworth for services and supplies. To counter this the valley turnpike was opened in 1821, a final attempt to reform Wirksworth's road network and preserve its trade. This is the present day Derby Road, constructed by linking existing roads and tracks running south from Wirksworth down the Ecclesbourne Valley via Bateman Bridge to Idridgehay. From Idridgehay a new route was built along the valley floor through the medieval parks of Shottle and Postern to reach Duffield village and join the main Derby turnpike, now the A6.

By the 1830s the pall of smoke, which had for years overhung the town from its industry, had dispersed as the lead, calamine and smelting mills had closed. Cheaper imported lead from Spain and Italy and the need and expense to 'unwater' the deeper lead veins by pumping and constructing underground soughs, drainage channels, had broken the local industry.

While lead production fell other industries in the town flourished, particularly textiles. The town had had a small woollen cloth industry since at least the 14th century, but it was not until after 1777 when Sir Richard Arkwright took over Haarlem Mill that textile manufacture gained importance. By 1815 cotton spinning had been replaced by tape weaving. The manufacture of tape and red tape in particular, used by government departments to tie up bundles of documents and files, became important. By the 1880s the town had five tape mills.

Another enterprise, slightly surprising in Wirksworth, was that of Charles Wright and Sons, wine and spirit merchants. They operated from premises on Coldwell Street, known as the Vaults, at present a paint and decorating shop. A large cellar and buildings stretched behind the premises, lost when Barmote Croft and the car park were constructed. From the late 18th century till the 1960s this whisky distillery provided jobs in the town blending and bottling their trade mark brands, Glen Haddon and Old Gran.

In China House Yard a short-lived china manufactury had flourished in the 1770s. It was possibly re-established after 1804 and produced some fine tea sets and similar ware decorated with a delicate flower pattern. The Wilson family later owned these premises and had a malting building on the site, constructed in 1820. In 1891 William Wilson conveyed this building to the Diocese of Southwell for use as a Sunday school and Parish Room.

A host of other trades were carried on in the town and surrounding hamlets including calico and stocking weaving, silk spinning, lace making, the manufacture of checks and ginghams, hat making, brick making, implement making, tanning, corn milling, stone cutting and banking. However none of these provided large-scale employment in the way the lead industry had.

By the 1840s Wirksworth was comparatively static relative to faster growing industrial towns, even though its population had increased by about a quarter in much the same period. It remained important for services to its immediate hinterland and its dependant villages, but its road network was described as the worst in the county. Only gradually did a new industry, limestone quarrying, develop to replace lead mining. To start with this was small scale, for the road problem was intractable and road transport expensive. The town did benefit to some extent from the opening of the Cromford and High Peak Railway in 1830 and this helped promote the quarry trade. However the line was not a great stimulus to trade in Wirksworth itself. It had been intended to carry coal by connecting two canals but it was slow and inefficient due to its many rope worked inclines. Wirksworth continued to suffer from relative isolation and the major developments of the first part of the railway age, the 'Railway Mania' of the 1840s again bypassed the town in favour of a route up the Derwent Valley. Wirksworth therefore did not receive a railway until 1867, too late to arrest its relative stasis in the early stages of the Industrial Revolution.

The arrival of the railway in the form of a branch line of the Midland Railway from Derby did finally provide an economic and social stimulus to the town. The route was used for carrying fresh milk to urban populations further south and limestone quarrying soon expanded with the advent of this cheap long distance rail haulage.

Limestone Quarrying

Limestone quarrying was the major industry of the town between the 1860s and 1989. Several quarries were opened and operated for various periods of time and provided much needed jobs for many of the town's workforce. Sadly this industry had more of a detrimental effect on the environment of the town than lead mining. Quarrying was noisy, dirty and dusty and a pall of dust covered Wirksworth every time quarry blasting took place, so much so that local people tell of the rivers of white water which ran down the drains every time it rained, washing the accumulated dust from the streets and house roofs into the sewers.

Dale Quarry

In 1862 Arthur Harward purchased an area of land around the Dale and bought some more in 1876. He began quarrying in 1874 calling his company the Wirksworth Dale Stone and Lime Company. In 1925, after several changes of ownership, it was bought by Wirksworth Quarries who eventually sold it to Tarmac Roadstone Ltd. It produced stone for concrete aggregates, the making of Tar-macadam and the extraction of sugar from sugar beet. It was linked by a standard gauge railway tunnel to the station, opened in 1877, which is still in existence but blocked at the quarry end. By 1965 it was producing 390,000 tons a year and employed 55 staff. This quarry closed in 1968 and can be crossed from a path at the top of the Dale.

Baileycroft Quarry

In 1871 George Colledge and John Keene leased an area to the west of North End from John Smith. This resulted in a small, short-lived quarry linked to the station yard by a narrow gauge tramway through two tunnels, one under North End and one under the garden of the railway stationmaster's house. The quarry closed in 1906 and part of the site is now the Fire Station and Co-op Store.

Middlepeak Quarry (Bowne and Shaws, and Hopton Wood Stone)

The lower level of Middlepeak, that is Stoneycroft Quarry, was begun in 1830 at the bottom and west side of Middleton Road by John Shaw who was a smallholder and lime burner. About 1870 he was joined by a Mr Bowne and the quarry was later known as Bowne and Shaws. A standard gauge railway connection was built in 1876 to a point just north of Cromford Road Bridge; this lasted until the quarry closed in 1989. The trackbed can be seen from Cromford Road bridge going west from the EVR line. There was also a narrow gauge tramway. In the centre, the upper level of Middlepeak, also Bowne and Shaw's, was connected by another narrow gauge tramway which crossed the Middleton Road on the level and passed down inclines to tip into trucks at what is now Ravenstor platform. The quarry was also joined to the railway by an overhead conveyor built in 1954 and dismantled in 2005.

The northernmost end of Middlepeak was initially owned by the Hopton Wood Company and joined the railway network at Middlepeak Wharf on the Cromford and High Peak Railway. In addition there was an aerial ropeway, out of use by 1920, which deposited stone into a tipping chute on the east side of where the Ravenstor platform now is. The quarry was employing 104 staff by 1965 and half of these men worked the lime-kilns. At this time it held a contract to supply stone for the Port Talbot Tidal Dock Scheme and supplied nearly half a million tons during the later years of the 1960s. Its principal output following this until its closure in 1989 was for roadstone aggregate.

Coal Hills Quarry (Hopton Wood Stone)

This quarry was on the north side of the Cromford and High Peak Railway, and is associated with a small hamlet of about 6 houses whose remains are in the grounds of the National Stone Centre. 24 people lived here in 1901 many employed in the quarry which was also adjacent to the Greymare Lead Mine.

Colehill Quarry (Alfred Shaw)

This quarry was on the south side of the Cromford and High Peak Railway and is associated with two adjacent quarries, Pensend and Steeple Grange Quarries. Serious production began in 1912 and continued into the late 1960s. From 1964 stone from this quarry was being extracted by George Wimpey Ltd. to build the M1 motorway. It was connected to the Wirksworth line by a narrow gauge tramway

Map 7: Wirksworth in 1835 taken from Sanderson's Map 'Twenty Miles round Mansfield'.

running down a steep incline from the quarry, near Old Lane Bridge to where Ravenstor platform is now. The path to the platform runs down this incline and some of the rails still exist beneath and next to the path. These quarries can be seen in the grounds of the National Stone Centre.

All these quarries closed over time, with Middlepeak, the last to remain in operation, closing in December 1989. Of the quarries around the Cromford and High Peak Railway, now the High Peak Trail, almost all of these became part of the National Stone Centre. Of the quarries nearer the town, both Middlepeak and Dale Quarry are quietly being taken over by nature. Baileycroft has partly been converted into Harrison Drive and Stoneycroft was granted by Tarmac to the town. This became a millennium project to convert it for community use. Local school children and other volunteers planted numerous trees here and voted to call it Stoney Wood. In 2005 a local artist, Aidan Shingler, had an idea to create a community meeting place at the top of the wood and he designed and found the funds for the Star Disc. Officially opened in 2011, this unique gathering place has wonderful views both during the day and at night and is much admired by residents and visitors to the town.

The Governance of the Town

Shortly after the arrival of the Railway, a new Town Hall was constructed by the Freemasons and opened in 1871. Until the creation of the Wirksworth Local Board in 1877 and then Wirksworth Urban District Council in 1895, the governance of the town was still mostly in the hands of the manorial courts and the Parish Vestry. In medieval times the ecclesiastical parish had kept records of births, marriages and deaths and by the 16th century had duties to upkeep the highways and offer relief for the poor. A Constable was appointed to be responsible for law and order and tax collection with two other officials, Surveyor of the Highways and Overseer of the Poor. The Parish Vestry Committee was effectively self-selecting and supervised by the vicar, churchwardens and other unelected local notables. The Vestry Committee's responsibilities, at least before the Reform Act of 1832, were for maintaining the church and its services, keeping the peace, repression of vagrancy, relief of destitution, mending of roads, suppression of nuisances, destruction of vermin, furnishing of soldiers, and even to some extent the enforcement of religious and moral discipline.

Records of the Wirksworth Vestry are largely missing; they were said, even in 1795, to be 'all over the town'. Its effectiveness shows occasionally however, for example in the provision of a Poor House in 1729 by the purchase of a house on Greenhill (Babington House), where it remained for at least a century. In the 1790s Joseph Branson is named as the Master of the Poor House. By the early 1800s the town was providing for 89 apprentices at the expense of parish rate-payers. This was considered to be a well-organised system and from what few records have survived the town's Vestry appeared to have been tolerably efficient. It was a bitter pill, when in 1840, the Charity Commissioners in London chose Belper to head the District's Poor Law Union, believing that Belper was better able to cope with the responsibility. Until the construction of the Town Hall, it is not recorded where the Vestry Committee met, probably in the church. The records of the rebuilding of St Mary's in 1870 note that the rebuilding, under Sir Gilbert Scott, had included plans for a new Vestry Room in the church, but this was no longer required and it was not built.

From the 18th century Wirksworth township formed a constabulary in its own right and had its own House of Correction, as has been seen earlier, built above Wash Green in 1791. Records held in the Derbyshire Record Office give details of prisoners and their offences. Between 1729 and 1913 over 400 cases were recorded for Wirksworth. These are mostly for stealing, burglary, assault or 'having a bastard child likely to be chargeable to the township'. In 1791 Francis Haynes was detained when found wandering for being 'an incorrigible rogue and vagabond', in 1798 Hannah Austin was said to have 'milked a cow and carried away milk' and in 1831 William Hall procured counterfeit money. In 1842 a house was built on North End for a magistrate and this remained a police house for a hundred years, before becoming a doctors' surgery. Known as 'The Old Lock up' it is at present a guest house and retains a police cell in the basement.

The Barmote Court

The Barmote Court is an extremely rare survival. These courts were present in all the Mercian Kingdom's provincial capitals and were called the Burgmote or Portmote Courts (there were various spelling differences, e.g. Burghmoot) and they may have been, in origin, those courts considered to be set up by Julius Agricola in the first century for the governance of Britain. The function of these Moot courts was primarily the regulation of trade and commerce and related town activities such as watch and ward. The difference between the Burghmote and the Portmote is considered by some writers to be that the Portmote Courts were found in those provincial capitals which supervised a mint and the Burghmote Courts were found in those provincial capitals which had no such supervision duties. By the 17th century in Barmaster Edward Manlove's time the Barmote Court had become so overwhelmed with lead mining issues that this was all that it thought it did. By then the Court only faintly remembered it once had other duties. It had long relinquished its other trade and commercial responsibilities, even the provision for apprentices fell to the Vestry to deal with.

The Court was unable to levy rates and this gradually constrained its work. It increasingly failed to engage in the town's wider business and its members did less and less even given their status as key citizens of the town. By the eighteenth century they thought their Court's only role was the regulation of lead mining, not the wider regulation of the town's commerce and the assurance of its dignity. For example the keeping of the Lead Miner's Measuring Dish in the Wirksworth Moot Hall was not a token of the court's role in the government of lead mining, but a token of the court's role in the regulation of weights and measures, almost all of which, by the eighteenth century, it had lost to the Court Leet. That the Wirksworth Court lost these roles had probably more to do with its being preoccupied by lead mining

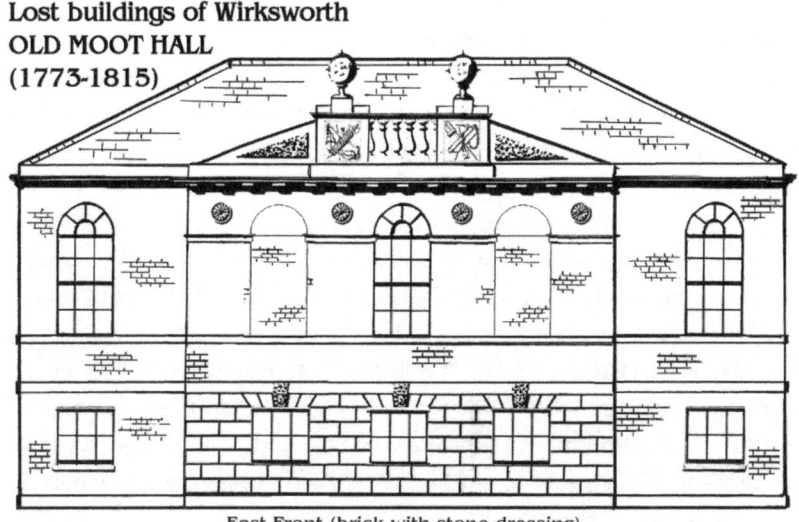

Lost buildings of Wirksworth
OLD MOOT HALL
(1773-1815)

East Front (brick with stone dressing)
Drawing by Anton Shone 2016

disputes than by any intention to lose them. It is now the only surviving Burgmoot Court in the country.

Religion, Health, Education, Social Life and Local Customs

St. Mary's continued as the parish church but nonconformity was also an important part of the life of the town. The earliest of the chapels, the Old Meeting Room or the Old Chapel was built on Coldwell Street in plain style with an attractive horseshoe gallery by the Presbyterians in 1700. This is now the United Reform chapel. Other chapels followed in the 19th century, a Wesleyan chapel on Chapel Lane in 1810, the Baptists in 1816, a Methodist chapel in the Dale built between 1828-30 and United Free Methodist Chapel on St. John's Street in 1886. Other chapels were built in Bolehill in 1823, at Warmbrook in 1846 and in Gorsey Bank at a similar time. At the same date the Roman Catholics were said to have formerly had a chapel in Wirksworth, described as a small square structure in St. John's Street built by the Beighton family but by then disused. A new Roman Catholic church was erected in 1931 in Gorsey Bank. A Temperance Hall was also built in Chapel Lane in 1860 to counter the growing number of public houses and alehouses.

In 1867 the Wirksworth Cottage Hospital was founded in Babington House by the efforts of Georgina Hurt. It had 22 beds and provision for three maternity patients. In 1927 Waltham House was bought, together with the adjacent cottage, for £1350 for use as a cottage hospital using legacies and donations from the townsfolk. A further sum was raised at the 1927 Carnival to furnish the hospital. This later became a maternity hospital and then Health Centre. It is now a Care Centre providing assisted living space for elderly people in the Wirksworth area.

Apart from the Grammar School, education in the town was provided by 'dame schools'. A Miss Stubbs ran a Lady's Boarding School in the town in the 1790s, and other similar establishments provided some day schools in the 19th century. A National School was built at the end of North End in 1851 and the Church of England opened one on North End in 1896. When the Grammar School moved to its new site on the Hannages in 1907 the old buildings in the churchyard were used as a cookery room and wood working site. The new buildings were designed by the architect George Widdows. He also designed the school buildings at New Bridge in the 1920's to an innovative cruciform plan as a Secondary Technical School. This is now Wirksworth Junior School.

Recreation in the town was provided by the annual fairs in September and weekly dances or musical events in the Assembly Room at the Red Lion Hotel. At the back of the Red Lion was a bowling green. This venue possibly also hosted Joseph Smedley's Travelling Theatre Company, known to have visited in 1812. Well Dressing re-started in Wirksworth in 1827, after piped water came to the town. This ancient custom may well reflect a pagan ritual in a limestone area where water frequently disappears at certain times of the year. Hackett, writing in 1863, said the tradition of well-dressing was kept at that time only in Derbyshire and in three locations: Buxton, Tissington and Wirksworth and 'in no others'.

Apart from a few nineteenth century buildings including the Town Hall, the Non-conformist chapels and the schools, the town retained the character of a provincial Georgian market town, dominated by winding alleys, and narrow streets with houses and shops zig-zagging up the hillsides.

Twentieth Century Wirksworth

Private residential housing took place after the first world war along Cromford Road and Derby Road and after the second world war local authority housing expanded the town at Snowfield View by Millhouses, King Edward Street on the Gilkin and King George Street at Pillow Butts. The most radical change to the centre of town occurred between 1938-40 when a new road, Harrison Drive, was blasted through the former Baileycroft quarry to open the way to Cromford. This necessitated restricting the Market Place to its present site and the demolition of a number of properties, including Doxey's Tearooms and Watts' taxi office.

Further expansion to the town took place in the 1950s when local authority housing was built on the east side of Derby Road and in the sixties on the west side. The Anthony Gell School was enlarged on its site on the Hannages in 1965 as the Grammar School became comprehensive. Further expansion of the town followed the sale of Yokecliff Farm in the 1970's with private development of the Yokecliff estate to the north of Summer Lane. South of Summer Lane local authority housing also expanded towards the Broadmeadow (Kings Field) Recreation Ground. Much of the older town centre property was in a poor state of repair by this time and declared a General Improvement Area by West Derbyshire District Council. In 1978 the Civic Trust chose the town for a pilot regeneration project leading to a Europa Nostra award in 1983. Many derelict properties were restored during this time, notably Hopkinson's House 1-3 Greenhill, 6-11 St. Mary's Gate and 31-33 The Dale.

Postcard of Coldwell Street and Gilkin, c.1900

Later residential development has been small scale and within the built-up area of the town.

An estate for light industry was developed on Derby Road on the site of a market garden and the bus garage and another to the west of Cromford Road during the 1980s leading to a revival of employment in the town, particularly small technology companies. The regeneration also attracted art and craft industries to establish in Wirksworth, for example metal working, woodwork, textiles and design work. One of the first of these, in the 1970s, was the high quality lingerie company Janet Reger, who had a small production workshop in West End. The end of large scale quarrying close to the town, together with the Clean Air Act in 1956, had a major effect on the environment, which improved significantly.

These improvements and influx of new ideas led to the start of the Wirksworth Festival Art & Architecture Trail in 1995 when a group of local artists opened their houses to show off their work. This has been running ever since and over a fortnight music, drama and dance events take place during the Festival. This is based around the time of year of the Clypping of the church, an ancient ceremony where the congregation hold hands around the church and sing 'We love the place O Lord in which thy honour dwells', a custom revived in 1921. It takes place on the nearest

Sunday to September 8th, the feast day of St. Mary the Virgin, to whom the church is dedicated.

The last twenty years have seen further steps taken to develop tourism. This started with the Steeple Grange Light Railway and was followed by Wirksworth Heritage Centre, the National Stone Centre, the Ecclesbourne Valley Railway and most recently the Northern Lights Cinema. All these attract visitors to the town whilst also providing amenities and interest for local people.

These changes brings us to the present day, for they enabled Wirksworth to develop into its modern guise with tourism, small technological companies and practical and professional services providing local employment and making the town an excellent place to live.

Conclusion

The Past, the Present and the Future

WIRKSWORTH'S ROLE HAS changed many times. Each time it has coped with that change and often pulled itself up by 'its own shoelaces'. The decline of the lead industry, and to a lesser extent agriculture, was accompanied by an almost concurrent rise in textile manufacture and limestone quarrying. The decline of these industries by the late 1980s saw an increasing reliance on services and small industry. A report commissioned by the town in 2006 found that 'a cluster of communities around Wirksworth was home to a prolific and exceptionally talented mix of innovative, imaginative and creative companies and individuals'.

Some residents are descendants of old Wirksworth families - people whose family names appear in the early rentals, others arrive to take up a job or retire here. Once here they usually stay and all of them, and those from the surrounding area, use the local services - health provision, local shopping, schools, the Leisure Centre, tradesmen and professional services.

In the last twenty years by a series of small steps tourists have arrived and they demand particular services – an increase in cafes and eating places, bed and breakfast and self-catering cottages. It is tourism in which Wirksworth has considerable strength, greater strength than most of our competitor towns. For Wirksworth is at the head of a fine lovely valley, the Ecclesbourne Valley, and the town boasts a range of tourist attractions. It has a wonderful character in terms of its built environment, situation and its inhabitants. Residents and visitors should all appreciate its past glory and future success.

Further Reading and Information

Websites

Wirksworth Parish Records: www.wirksworth.org.uk
Wirksworth Archaeological Society: www.wirksworthromanproject.com

Books

Ancient Peakland, Bevan B., 2007
Around Wirksworth, Eardley D., 1998
Derbyshire Parish Churches, Leonard J., 1993
Mercia and the making of England, Walker I.W., 2000
Lead Miner's Heyday, Slack R., 2000
O'er Back and on the Hillock: The Dale and Greenhill, Wirksworth, Doxey, J., 1989
The Wirksworth Branch, Sprenger H., 2004
Wirksworth and five miles around, Hackett R. H., 1863, reprinted 1991
Wirksworth in old picture postcards, Holmes T., 2000
Wirksworth: Picturing Past & Present, Richards, P., 2010
Wirksworth Pottery, Tudor, T.L., 1916
The Wirksworth Story, New Life for an Old Town, Mitchell, G., The Civic Trust, 1989

Articles

A Survey of the Soake and Manor of Wirksworth 1649, Arkwright Rev., Derbyshire Archaeological Journal, 1912
Lost towns of Roman Britain, 2: Lutudarum, Branigan K., Popular Archaeology, September, 1985
The name of Lutudarum, Derbyshire, Breeze A., Britannia, Vol 33, 2002
The Wirksworth Slab, Cockerton R.W., Derbyshire Archaeological Journal, 1962
Urbanisation and the middling sorts in Derbyshire market towns: Ashbourne and Wirksworth, 1660-1830, Dack C.N., Leicester University thesis, 2010

The Iconography of the Wirksworth Slab, Kurth B., Burlington Magazine, 1945

Medieval Fairs and Markets and the Wirksworth Charter, Marcombe D., Fleming Press, 2006

Geographical Aspects of the Development of Wirksworth from the Beginning of the NineteenthCentury to the Present (1800-1965), Ottrey F.S., University of Nottingham thesis, 1966

The Derbyshire Portway: An archaeological assessment, Shone A. and Smart D., 2012

Derbyshire Extensive Urban Survey: Wirksworth, Archaeological Assessment Report, Stroud G., Derbyshire County Council 2001

Documents

Map of the Gell Estate, Wirksworth, 1709: Derbyshire Record Office, Matlock, D258 M/18/6/14

Survey of houses, barns, gardens in Wirksworth, The estate of the Hon. Sir Philip Gell. 1710. Derbyshire Record Office, Matlock, D1892 Z/Z1, copy from Wirksworth Parish Magazine, 1899

Tithe Map of Wirksworth, 1837: Derbyshire Record Office, Matlock, D2360 3/129

Rental, 1415: The National Archives, DL 42/4

Rental, 1420: Derbyshire Record Office, Matlock, D258/16/18

Rental, 1473: The National Archives, SC11/159

Parliamentary Survey, 1649: The National Archives, E317/Derb/28

List of Illustrations

Illustrations and Maps within the Text

Wirksworth Stone
Wirksworth Sceat
Wirksworth Charter 835
Pack horses
Brassington Lane
Wirksworth churchyard
Market Place
Cruck cottage
Wirksworth Hall
Nether House
Wirksworth china teapot
Old Moot Hall
Coldwell Street

Map 1: Wirksworth today
Map 2: The Mercian Province of the Peak
Map 3: Wirksworth Area showing early place-names, tracks, burial mounds and archaeological find sites
Map 4: Medieval Wirksworth
Map 5: Gorsey Bank in 1879 from 1st edition OS 6" map
Map 6: Survey of Sir Philip Gell's estate in Wirksworth 1710
Map 7: Wirksworth in 1835 taken from Sanderson's Map 'Twenty Miles round Mansfield'

Illustrations and maps reproduced with permission from Anthony Short, Anton Shone, Mary Wiltshire, Derbyshire Record Office and Wirksworth Heritage Centre.